PEACE AND VIOLENCE
IN THE ETHICS OF
DIETRICH BONHOEFFER

PEACE AND VIOLENCE IN THE ETHICS OF DIETRICH BONHOEFFER

AN ANALYSIS OF METHOD

Trey Palmisano

FOREWORD BY
Reinhard Krauss

WIPF & STOCK · Eugene, Oregon

PEACE AND VIOLENCE IN THE ETHICS OF
DIETRICH BONHOEFFER
An Analysis of Method

Copyright © 2016 Trey Palmisano. All rights reserved. Except for brief quotations in critical publications or reviews, no part of this book may be reproduced in any manner without prior written permission from the publisher. Write: Permissions. Wipf and Stock Publishers, 199 W. 8th Ave., Suite 3, Eugene, OR 97401.

Wipf & Stock
An Imprint of Wipf and Stock Publishers
199 W. 8th Ave., Suite 3
Eugene, OR 97401

www.wipfandstock.com

ISBN 13: 978-1-62032-653-4

Manufactured in the U.S.A.   12/23/2015

For Krista, Isabelle, Lexi, and Sam.
Your love is my peace and comfort.

Contents

Foreword by Reinhard Krauss | ix
Acknowledgments | xiii
Introduction | xv
Abbreviations | xxi
Timeline | xxiii

1 Influences in Bonhoeffer's Ethical Thought | 1
2 Bonhoeffer's Ethical Method | 31
3 Bonhoeffer and the Quest for Peace | 66
4 Bonhoeffer and the Question of Murder | 107

Bibliography | 147
Index | 157

Foreword

AN ANALYSIS OF DIETRICH Bonhoeffer's position on peace and violence is of important significance both for advancing historical research and as a major test case to illuminate Bonhoeffer's unique approach to Christian ethics. But it is at the same time more than that. In the context of the contemporary debate on issues such as the moral justification of war and its conduct, methods employed in the fight against terrorism, including torture and extrajudicial killings by state agencies, and possible limits on the right to own firearms in efforts to reduce gun violence, the following monograph also touches on key ethical problems that are of crucial import both for the United States and for our increasingly interconnected and interdependent world.

Trey Palmisano lays out an impressive foundation for his investigation by tracing the sometimes overt and sometimes very subtle influences other theologians, ethicists, and philosophers exerted on Bonhoeffer's own thinking. In each case, Bonhoeffer emerges as an informed yet thoroughly independent thinker in conversation with a broad array of other approaches. He is free to adopt certain insights of others yet is never captured by any one of the established ethical models as he critically and constructively develops his own unique understanding of Christian ethics and its implication for the central issues of peace and violence.

One of the much debated questions is whether Bonhoeffer's thinking on peace and violence changed substantively over time. Does Bonhoeffer's participation in the conspiracy represent a break or at least a significant modification of a reputed earlier commitment to a pacifist stance? Or does his ethical approach, both conceptually and as expressed in his actions, present an internally consistent and unbroken trajectory throughout the course of Bonhoeffer's life? The author of this monograph clearly and emphatically argues for the latter view. With notable attention to detail, he assembles an impressive array of sources to make a persuasive case for the fundamental internal consistency of Bonhoeffer's ethical position on peace and violence from his early days as a young pastoral candidate serving the German-speaking congregation in Barcelona, Spain to the mature theologian and ethical thinker confined to a small cell in Tegel prison. Significantly, the supporting evidence is drawn from across the entire Bonhoeffer opus, ranging from Bonhoeffer's explicitly theological and ethical works to his lesser-known, more informal writings, such as his sermons and letters.

The study identifies Bonhoeffer's unwavering commitment to a relational Christological ethics as the linchpin which lends internal consistency to his ethical stance on peace and violence from his early writings through his engagement with pacifism during his studies at Union Theological Seminary, the time of his famous sermon at Fanö, and all the way to the period of his involvement in the conspiracy and work on his *Ethics*. In an emphatic departure from ethical models based on absolute moral principles, Bonhoeffer rejects any approach as fundamentally flawed and inappropriate for a Christian ethics which seeks to identify human actions categorically along the spectrum of good and evil. Over the course of Bonhoeffer's theological development, his conceptual ethical framework shifts from an emphasis on obedience to Christ's command to a focus on the ethical category of responsibility without ever losing its mooring in a relational ethics of following the living Christ in the concrete situation of the here and now.

In our age of nuclear proliferation, unconventional warfare, and the potential for conflict and unprecedented military destruction on a global scale, today's ethical issues concerning peace and violence are different from those Bonhoeffer was facing in his

Foreword

particular historical context. However, in the quest for a peaceful future of humanity, Bonhoeffer's clarion call for a Christian ethics grounded not in abstract principles but in a concrete situational and communal matrix bound to the living Christ is a proposal as compelling and worth serious reflection and consideration today as it was in Bonhoeffer's time. In allowing us to hear Bonhoeffer's voice anew in both its clarity and nuanced complexity, this study is an important contribution to a most vital debate.

Reinhard Krauss

Lecturer, Center for the Study of Religion
University of California, Los Angeles
February 1, 2013

Acknowledgments

I WOULD LIKE TO extend my heartfelt thanks to Dr. Stephen Vicchio who encouraged the publication of this present work. He was the first professor with whom I had a class at the Ecumenical Institute of Theology (St. Mary's Seminary & University) and was the last professor I worked with prior to graduation. Thanks to Drs. Michael J. Gorman and Brian Berry for their early readings of this manuscript, and Dr. Anthony Hunt who invited me to share my research in 2013 with his graduate students who were taking a class on Dietrich Bonhoeffer at the Ecumenical Institute of Theology and asked more than a few engaging questions. Drs. James Patrick Kelley and Philip Ziegler offered valuable insights that were considered in the final version of this manuscript, while conversations with Dr. Peter C. Hoffmann and Giles MacDonogh provided important historical context on Bonhoeffer's Germany. I am also indebted to Betty Bolden, Reader Services for Rare Books and Archives at The Burke Library at Union Theological Seminary, who helped with many requests for access to the Bonhoeffer collection by sending along countless copies of archived materials to me.

I would also like to thank Dr. Reinhard Krauss for our conversations by telephone and email, which began in 2011, as well as for writing the foreword to this book. His years involved with the translation of the Bonhoeffer Works Series into English made him an invaluable resource. A special thanks to Drs. Victoria J. Barnett and Thomas Culbertson for making introductions to those working in the field of Bonhoeffer studies, while taking time out of their busy schedules to advise a junior scholar. I am grateful and humbled.

Introduction

DIETRICH BONHOEFFER'S INFLUENCE ON Christianity is profound. Indeed, John D. Godsey writes candidly how "his influence cuts across our customary theological, denominational, national, and age-group divisions."[1] For conservatives, Bonhoeffer remains a person of faith, who, despite questionable activity in a plot to eliminate Adolf Hitler, was nevertheless willing to lay down his life in a pious act of martyrdom. Stephen R. Haynes writes, "Most evangelicals are aware of Bonhoeffer's participation in a violent coup against Hitler. Although they may find this decision troubling, they view it as one made in a situation of extreme duress by a man engaged in mortal conflict with the epitome of human evil."[2] For liberals, he is a persuasive example of Christianity in conversation with the culture. "Concern for the church's role in society is a dimension of Bonhoeffer's legacy," asserts Haynes, and one that "has received particular attention from liberals," mentioning Geffrey B. Kelly, Larry Rasmussen, and Keith W. Clement, among others.[3] With his interest in and service to the public square, Bonhoeffer's insights are remembered for binding together the sacred and the secular into a theological interpretation of the world.

Yet despite his influence among conservatives and liberals, Bonhoeffer is also dissentingly rejected. Those with a conservative

---

1. Godsey, *Preface to Bonhoeffer: The Man and Two of His Shorter Writings*, 7.
2. Haynes, *The Bonhoeffer Phenomenon: Portraits of a Protestant Saint*, 94.
3. Ibid., 38.

INTRODUCTION

commitment to Scripture as the inspired word of God see his threat in the rejection of inveterate interpretations of key doctrinal points.[4] Among liberals, representatives of feminism, reject, for example, his promotion of spiritual hierarchy within the family. Judith Plaskow references Bonhoeffer's "Wedding Sermon from a Prison Cell" (May 1943) as an "appalling statement" of the theological images and attitudes towards women in modern theology.[5] Even Rowan Williams, recalling Bonhoeffer studies in the 1960s, laments his adaptation by Anglicans.[6] Those who have turned Bonhoeffer into a saint exemplifying the heroic motif of the Christian life in his uncompromising stand for Christ might be puzzled by Karl Barth's critique of the young Lutheran pastor as a "deep and disturbing man," a judgment no doubt that arose from points of misunderstanding that derived from Bonhoeffer's own actions, which included his exodus from Germany to pursue pastoral work abroad at a time when the German church was in turmoil.[7] Furthermore, interest and challenges generated by Bonhoeffer readings have resulted in numerous papers, monographs, and lectures. Richard Weikart, focusing primarily on Bonhoeffer's interpretation among evangelicals, makes this point in his article "So Many Different Dietrich Bonhoeffers," a title which speaks to the problem of interpretation that regularly accompanies Bonhoeffer studies.[8] This work itself is only one such attempt.

---

4. An example of this is a review offered by Weikart on Eric Metaxas' recent biography *Bonhoeffer: Pastor, Martyr, Prophet, Spy* (2010), in which he charges Metaxas with making Bonhoeffer an evangelical conservative. See Weikart, "Metaxas' Counterfeit Bonhoeffer: An Evangelical Critique," http://www.csustan.edu/history/faculty/weikart/metaxas.htm (accessed March 12, 2012).

5. Plaskow, *The Coming of Lilith: Essays on Feminism, Judaism, and Sexual Ethics, 1972–2003*, 42.

6. On the problem of Bonhoeffer's interpretation in the Anglican community, Williams writes, "We made him an Anglican and a liberal Anglican at that" ("Bonhoeffer, the Sixties, and After: Consultation on Bonhoeffer: Britain and British Theology," 1).

7. Smith, *World Come of Age: A Symposium on Dietrich Bonhoeffer*, 131.

8. Weikart, "So Many Different Bonhoeffers," 69–81.

Introduction

Yet interest in Bonhoeffer continues to stem from the extraordinary circumstances of his life: a child growing up in the aftermath of one war who would carve out his theology in the rising tide of another war. In this context, his insights resonate through the indispensible autobiographical dimension to his theology, so much that W. A. Visser 't Hooft questions, "Is not this hunger and thirst for reality, for becoming incarnate, for living the Christian life and not merely talking about it the real key to Bonhoeffer's message?"[9] Yet some argue that his circumstances overshadow his theology for good reason. Ann L. Nickson writes how Bonhoeffer has been regarded by some "as a theological lightweight who owes his fame to the tragic circumstances of his death rather than to the depth of originality of his theological insight."[10] Bonhoeffer often gets lost in the long shadow created by Barth, Bultmann, and Brunner, and as Godsey notes, his "thought has not been taken with due seriousness in his own country."[11] Nevertheless, where attraction remains, it is precisely with attention to "his unusual combination of thought and action."[12] Yet this unity of theology and practice is a result not of the heavy thinking done in such works as *Act and Being*, but in a move to ethics which at times appeared both fortuitous, with regard to his early preparation and thinking on ethical issues, and essential, given the terrible events that would overtake all of Germany.

The question of Bonhoeffer's pacifism is as important to the history of scholarship deriving from his work as it remains in popular culture, and requires careful explication to avoid rupturing the closely knit fabric of his work. Two readings of his pacifism bring the issue into relief. The first suggests that Bonhoeffer goes through a period where his theology moves in the direction of peaceful nonviolence by way of a firm commitment to social ethics, culminating in the early 1930s when he is entrenched in

---

9. Haynes, *The Bonhoeffer Phenomenon: Portraits of a Protestant Saint*, 6.
10. Nickson, *Bonhoeffer on Freedom: Courageously Grasping Reality*, 1.
11. Godsey, "Bonhoeffer for the Eighties: A Report on the Oxford 1980 Conference and an Outlook for the Decade Ahead," 3.
12. Bethge, *Dietrich Bonhoeffer: A Biography*, xiii.

Introduction

Christian pacifism to the exclusion of all violence. As Hitler's power and menace increase, and the prospect of peaceful resolution grows increasingly dim, Bonhoeffer is forced to judge against his own conscience and make the choice to participate in a *Putsch* against Hitler. Such a position is typified in the following comment by Miroslav Volf: "It may be that consistent nonretaliation and nonviolence will be impossible in the world of violence. Tyrants may need to be taken down from their thrones and the madmen stopped from sowing desolation. Dietrich Bonhoeffer's decision to take part in an attempt to assassinate Hitler is a well-known and persuasive example of such thinking."[13] A second reading looks to rework what it means to be a pacifist. This view suggests that peace became the core Christian conviction of Bonhoeffer during the early 1930s, and that despite his advocacy of violence against Hitler as the drums of war grew louder, violence should not be absolutized as the antithesis of peace. Pacifism involves space for a less acute rejection of violence.

The position I want to argue in this thesis rejects the all-too-easy dichotomy between peace and violence and argues that the proper approach to Bonhoeffer's ethics comes by way of a *methodological analysis* rather than through specific ethical responses that often appear to contradict rather than complement and therefore must be redefined. Rasmussen's assertion that "both pacifism and conspiracy must somehow flow together" is instructive in this regard.[14] This flowing together, however, is not rooted in a dialectical approach or a particular response in which violence need only be fitted into a re-worked definition of peace. Rather, this flowing together can only be understood as activity derived in a method that has Christ at the center. Where Bonhoeffer's method *is* refined to add new perspective, it continues to maintain character features that do not rely on pacifism or violence as necessary expressions. Peace, like violence, is the outward evidence of an ethic in operation whose movement is continually directed and reshaped in a

---

13. Volf, *Exclusion and Embrace: a Theological Exploration of Identity, Otherness, and Reconciliation*, 306.

14. Rasmussen, *Dietrich Bonhoeffer: Reality and Resistance*, 95.

INTRODUCTION

relational experience of Christ. In making these claims, I affirm that Bonhoeffer should not be labeled a pacifist, but not entirely for the same reasons.

The quest for a method does not come without a caution. As Rasmussen notes, "the student intent upon uncovering Bonhoeffer's method in ethics is greeted with both literary and intellectual fragmentation."[15] But this caution need not preclude any and all conclusions. While we must analyze the writings of a developing theologian from *Sanctorum Communio* into *Discipleship* and alongside the writing of his unfinished *Ethics*, neither Rasmussen nor any other scholar who labors in Bonhoeffer's studies is undermined in discovering persistent themes, even where fragmentation occurs.[16] Rasmussen himself asserts that Bonhoeffer has methodological criteria that run throughout his works.[17] Yet, in Bonhoeffer's own self-assessment of his work during the years of 1928-1931, which corresponds to what some scholars believe represents his move from a justification of violence to a firm commitment to non-violence, he remained a consistent thinker.[18] It is the goal of this work to explore whether Bonhoeffer's own assessment proved accurate through an analysis of method.

The composition of this work is structured as follows. In chapter 1, I will examine thinkers who were influential with respect to Bonhoeffer's ethics. While not everyone is included, the choice of these examples represents those whose influence can fill the footprint of his ethical development. In chapter 2, I will examine the way in which Bonhoeffer develops his own method by examining examples among his various genres of writing, all of which offer important insights, since, to quote Godsey, "people

---

15. Rasmussen, "A Question of Method," 105.
16. One such study is Nickson's *Bonhoeffer on Freedom*.
17. Rasmussen, *Dietrich Bonhoeffer: Reality and Resistance*, 115.
18. Bonhoeffer commented on a phone call received by Max Diestel in December 1927 asking whether he wanted to go to Barcelona, an experience which Bonhoeffer recalls "set his entire thinking on a track from which it has not yet deviated and never will." Interestingly, he considers this experience his first encounter with ecumenical Christianity (*DBWE* 16, 1/207, 367).

INTRODUCTION

now have a vital interest in every word Bonhoeffer wrote."[19] Chapter 3 will examine Bonhoeffer's interest in pacifism, and how his pacifism operated with reference to his methodology. Chapter 4 concerns the question of murder, in which I will analyze Bonhoeffer's early attitudes to violence and his later work during his time as a conspirator and double agent in the *Abwehr*. Because the question of war is often tied to the question of peace in chapter 3, I will at times revisit examples analyzed, howbeit along different lines. At the conclusion of chapter 4, I will briefly speak to the observations attempted in this work.

---

19. Godsey, "Reading Bonhoeffer in English Translation: Some Difficulties," 86.

Abbreviations

DBW   *Dietrich Bonhoeffer Werke (German)*

DBWE   *Dietrich Bonhoeffer Works (English)*

NRS   *No Rusty Swords: Letters, Lectures, and Notes 1928–1936*

When citing passages in the footnotes from the German edition, I have referred to the volume and section separated by a colon. When citing passages in the footnotes from the English edition, I have referred to the volume, section, and page number (where appropriate) separated by commas. If a volume is not arranged with sections, I refer only to the volume and page number.

Timeline

The following timeline is made available to orient readers to important periods in Dietrich Bonhoeffer's professional and academic life.

1923 – Bonhoeffer studies theology at Tübingen University.

1924 – Bonhoeffer studies theology at University of Berlin. He travels to Italy and North Africa.

1927 – Bonhoeffer graduates from University of Berlin and receives doctorate at age 21. His doctoral dissertation, *Sanctorum Communio*, is celebrated by Karl Barth as a "theological miracle."

1928 – Bonhoeffer is assigned to a German congregation in Barcelona, Spain as a curate.

1929 – Bonhoeffer returns to Berlin and works in the theology department at Berlin; works on his *Habilitationsschrift Act and Being*.

1930 – Bonhoeffer travels to Union Theological Seminary in New York to study for a year.

1931 – Bonhoeffer returns to Germany as lecturer in theology at the University of Berlin. He is appointed youth secretary to the World Alliance for Promoting International Friendship through the Churches. He receives his ordination at St. Matthew's Church in Berlin.

Timeline

1933 – Bonhoeffer co-drafts the Bethel Confession with Hermann Sasse as a statement of faith opposing the national Reich church. The National Synod approves the Aryan paragraph, preventing Jews and "Non-Aryans" from holding church positions. Bonhoeffer takes a position in London at two German-speaking congregations.

1934 – The Confessing church adopts the Barmen Confession drafted by Karl Barth. Bonhoeffer attends an ecumenical conference at Fanö, Denmark, where he delivers his well-known peace lecture.

1935 – Bonhoeffer heads up seminary at Zingsthof, but later relocates to Finkenwalde. He begins work on *Discipleship*.

1936 – Bonhoeffer is prevented from teaching at the University of Berlin. He is labeled a "pacifist and enemy of the State."

1937 – Finkenwalde is shut down on order of Heinrich Himmler. Bonhoeffer publishes *Discipleship*.

1938 – Bonhoeffer is prohibited to remain in Berlin. He makes his first contact with the German resistance.

1939 – Bonhoeffer receives an invitation to the United States but remains only for a month, expressing his need to return to Germany. He becomes involved with the *Abwehr*.

1940 – Bonhoeffer is ordered to make regular reports to the local Gestapo offices. He begins writing *Ethics* and continues covert work with the *Abwehr*, making contacts abroad.

1941 – Bonhoeffer is prohibited from publishing. He visits various locations abroad to gain support for the German resistance until the auspices of intelligence gathering.

1943 – Bonhoeffer is arrested on the charge of subversion and remanded to Tegel Prison in Berlin.

1944 – The Gestapo discovers files linking Bonhoeffer to activities against the Führer. His brother Klaus and brother-in-law Rüdiger

Timeline

Schleicher are arrested. Bonhoeffer is relocated to Prinz Albrecht Strasse Prison in Berlin.

1945 – Bonhoeffer is moved to various locations including Buchenwald, Regensburg, Schönberg, and eventually Flossenbürg where on April 9th, he is executed. He was 39 years old.

1

Influences in Bonhoeffer's Ethical Thought

ASSESSING THE WORK OF thinkers who have had an impact on Dietrich Bonhoeffer is an important step toward understanding the development of his method. Influence, however, is not always a matter of direct citation. It may also be determined by the author's own lack of originality. In such cases, influence may be reconstructed as an engagement between an author and another party whose identity is ascertained by the nature of the problem under consideration and the solution offered. Martin Rumscheidt provides the following direction: "It is when one studies the thoughts that Bonhoeffer presents as his own, the positions he defends and his life, that one discerns who influenced him and how."[1] In this chapter, I focus on five thinkers and the way each influenced Bonhoeffer's work in ethics.

Martin Luther

Germany was not just coaxed into modernity by Martin Luther; for all intents and purposes modern Germany was founded by him. "Researchers of the German language are to a great extent agreed that Luther, not only with his translation of the Bible but also with his prefaces to the Bible, sermons, Small Catechism, and his

---

1. Rumscheidt, "Significance of Adolf von Harnack and Reinhold Seeberg," 202.

songs, pamphlets, and tracts, is an event in the history of German literature to which no other can be compared."[2] Indeed, Jörg Rades writes, "Luther not only influenced German theology but German language and the German political attitude . . . Luther is present in many areas of life unknown to many. The impact of his life helped Luther to disappear in the anonymity of the 'Zeitgeist.'"[3] This observation is certainly true for Bonhoeffer, who at times adopts Luther's thinking as an almost self-evident reality in his writing.

From early in Bonhoeffer's student days in Berlin, writes Heinz Eduard Tödt, "Martin Luther's theology decisively influenced Bonhoeffer."[4] During his own days as a professor in Berlin, Bonhoeffer exhorted his own students to "go back to the beginning, to our wellsprings, to the true Bible, to the true Luther."[5]

One important agreement with Luther derived from his sermon entitled "Sermon von den guten Werken" (1520), stressing that all ethics begin with God. Luther writes "*Das erste und höchste, alleredelste gute Werk ist der Glaube an Christum . . .*"[6] That the first commandment was considered by Luther to be the greatest ethical duty imposed upon humanity, and that love, which draws a relational rather than formal bond between Christ and the disciple, is irrevocably etched into the reality of Bonhoeffer's theology.

This emphasis on love as the first and greatest work, expressed as faith born in humanity by God, makes the remaining commandments secondary.[7] As Rades notes, "In the end, it seems that in a rather unexpected way the whole of ethics in Luther's understanding cannot be set apart from the doctrine of justification. It stands in dialectical relation with it where faith is

---

2. Bayer, "Luther as Interpreter of Holy Scripture," 73.
3. Rades, "Luther and Bonhoeffer," 3.
4. Ibid., 4.
5. *DBWE* 12, 2/17, 435.
6. "The first and highest, noblest good work is faith in Christ" (my translation). (Luther, *Die reformatorischen Grundschriften*, § 54).
7. *DBWE* 12, 3/1, 444–45.

Influences in Bonhoeffer's Ethical Thought

regarded as the first of the good works."[8] This concept is essential to Bonhoeffer's method.[9] Luther's influence can also be discovered in the way in which Bonhoeffer translated certain of Luther's doctrines as ethical interpretations.[10] Tödt asserts this is particularly true in Bonhoeffer's use of *Stellvertretung*, a theme he sustains from "his dissertation to his latest manuscript for an ethics."[11] Hans Friedrich Daub asserts that the importance of the concept to works like *Discipleship* is self-evident. *"Breiten Raum nimmt in Nachfolge ein genuin lutherisches Stellvertretungsdenken ein. Bonhoeffer schreibt von der Unumgänglichkeit, die Sünder wegen ihre Sünde zu bestrafen, und von der stellvertretend erlittenen Strafe Christi am Kreuz."*[12]

Clifford J. Green describes the concept in Bonhoeffer as follows:

> Christ the Stellvertreter is the initiator and reality of the new humanity. The person and action of Christ is "vicarious" in that he does for human beings what they cannot possibly do for themselves ... as Kollektivperson, from Adam; every member of humanity sins in the same

---

8. Rades, "Luther and Bonhoeffer," 12.

9. An important problem remains that cannot be addressed in this work; namely, whether faith is a product of human action or divine action. In the introduction to *Discipleship*, the English editors remark that "Although in the doctrine of justification the coupling of faith in Christ with obedience to Christ suggests a theological sequence from faith to obedience, the two can never be separated chronologically" (*DBWE* 4, 5). Rades asserts that Bonhoeffer creates a tension by suggesting both options in the *Discipleship* ("Luther and Bonhoeffer," 13-15). Heinrich Traugott Vogel sees the process as two steps in which faith is created in the individual, followed by the individual acting in faith (*Christus als Vorbild und Versöhner*, 297). Rades notes that this brings Bonhoeffer no closer to Luther.

10. Krötke notes that ethics for Bonhoeffer was nothing other than applied Christology ("Dietrich Bonhoeffer and Martin Luther," 60).

11. Tödt, *Authentic Faith*, 7 (cf. Weissbach, "Christology and Ethics," 100-101, and von Soosten in *DBWE* 1, 303).

12. "A genuine Lutheran thinking of representation occupies considerable space in *Discipleship*. Bonhoeffer wrote of the inevitability of sinners being punished because of their sins, and of the punishment of Christ, which was suffered vicariously on the cross" (my translation). (Daub, *Die Stellvertretung*, 389).

3

way as Adam, but only Christ overcomes the "broken community" of sin.[13]

The result of this, writes Tödt, is that "no one should still say they are supposed to stand up for their own guilt on their own and alone."[14] And because of this, the individual is freed to love others the way Christ loved him.

The concept is often considered within systematics as an example of dogmatics in the realm of atonement theology. But Bonhoeffer's interest spans beyond its typical meaning. "Like Karl Barth, Bonhoeffer regards dogmatics and ethics as a unity, following the tradition of Reformation theology."[15] While the confessional dimension of Christ's vicarious substitution for the sins of humanity is a starting point, Bonhoeffer is much more concerned with how *Stellvertretung* presents itself in the world as an ethical concept.[16]

The connection between representation and incarnation was indispensable. Daub writes, *"Menschwerdung und Stellvertretung werden von Bonhoeffer in direktem Zusammenhang gesehen."*[17] For Bonhoeffer, one encounters God in the doctrines of the incarnation and atonement relationally rather than propositionally. Here too, Luther's influence is palpable. Bonhoeffer rejected the radical transcendence of Barth's God who was inaccessible to human effort. For Barth, even where Christ comes to reveal himself as the *Logos* of God, it is still only Christ *as* the infinite expression of God.[18] Bonhoeffer, however, rejected God's hiddenness as the wrong message. Eberhard Bethge writes, "Bonhoeffer vigorously

---

13. Green, *Bonhoeffer*, 56.
14. Tödt, *Authentic Faith*, 6.
15. Weissbach, "Christology and Ethics," 97.
16. As Moe-Lobeda writes, representation for Bonhoeffer (or "deputyship" in *Ethics*) meant both "standing on behalf of the persecuted, and assuming the guilt of the Western world" ("A Theology of the Cross," 299, n. 33).
17. "For Bonhoeffer, becoming human and representation are seen in direct connection" (my translation). (Daub, *Die Stellvertretung*, 438).
18. Webster, *Cambridge Companion to Karl Barth*, 53.

protests with Luther against this all his life . . . God's glory is total freedom not from, but for man."[19]

For Luther, the divine attributes (*communicatio idiomatum*) could be abstracted to the person of Jesus. The human nature was thus suffused with divinity. While concerns about the doctrine of God's impassibility and the meaning of *kenosis* (i.e., the emptying of the divine attributes in the fully human Christ) raise serious questions, Bonhoeffer saw in Luther's *finitum capax infinitum* the opportunity to drive home the idea of God drawing humanity to himself against the extra-Calvinisticum position of *finitum non capax infiniti* of which Barth was an adherent.

Just as Bonhoeffer found an ally in Luther on his view of community, so too Bonhoeffer's view of sacramental Christology was informed by Luther's view of the Lord's Supper as *Christus praesens*, expressed in "The Blessed Sacrament of the Holy and True Body of Christ, and the Brotherhoods" (1519). Here, the present Christ implicates our own *being-for-each-other* just as he meets us in the sacrament.[20] For Bonhoeffer, the soteriological dimension of the Lord's Supper is also reimagined ethically, in which he also sees himself tracking with Luther. The forgiveness of sins is not about participation in the mystery of sacrament; but, rather, by coming together as the community of Christ we become Christ for one another "for the mutual forgiveness of sins."[21] To paraphrase Rades, Bonhoeffer is concerned with who is in the sacrament rather than how he is in it.[22] The "who" becomes the coordinating principle and it draws upon the community to answer this question together. In *Sanctorum Communio: A Theological Study of the Sociology of the Church*, Bonhoeffer cites an example of this in a sermon by Luther in which he speaks of how the mystery of Holy Communion brings the community together. Here, an ethical reality emerges when one considers how Christ's love toward

---

19. Bethge, "Challenge of Bonhoeffer's Life and Theology," 37.
20. *DBWE* 1, 182.
21. Ibid., 184.
22. Rades, "Luther and Bonhoeffer," 20.

us requires that he take on the burden of humanity, which in turn demands that we burden ourselves with one another.[23]

Bonhoeffer takes up this point again in 1933, during his lectures in Berlin. Bonhoeffer sees in Luther's rejection of the doctrine of transubstantiation Luther's own appreciation of *Christus praesens* as revelation for us.[24] Quoting Luther, he writes, "It is merely for the sake of revelation. He is everywhere. But you will not catch him unless he offers himself to you and he himself gives the bread meaning for you through his Word."[25] The Lord's Supper is a meeting place for the community understood first as an ethical reality. The concrete sacrament reminds us that Jesus is a brother alongside many brothers and sisters. It calls us together as embodied believers just as it expresses Christ's body. In this way, the Lord's Supper becomes a twofold spiritual-body experience through the celebration of Christ who does the work of God, and the fellowship of believers that comes together bodily in one spirit. In the Berlin lectures, Bonhoeffer expresses the ethical reality of this concept as existential transformation. When a believer takes in Christ, his orientation becomes "Christ for others" in the same way Bonhoeffer asserts the bread and wine formed through Christ become "being-for-the-person," no longer having meaning in themselves. The essential orientation of the individual toward others means that one cannot do ethics outside of this fundamental orientation. Christ is *pro me / pro nobis*. Daphne Hampson notes that Luther's influence on Bonhoeffer here, in which Christ is not simply *Objekt*, but object of faith, while mediated through Søren Kierkegaard, is evident.[26]

One of Luther's most discussed doctrines is that of the two kingdoms (*Zwei-Reiche-Lehre*). William John Wright notes that in contemporary times, Nazism was the predominant influence for the

---

23. *DBWE* 1, 178–79.

24. Bonhoeffer, however, rejects Luther's explanation on the question of "how" Christ is in the Lord's Supper, calling it "impossible metaphysical hypostatizations." *DBWE* 12, 2/12, 321.

25. Ibid.

26. Hampson, *Christian Contradictions*, 23.

Influences in Bonhoeffer's Ethical Thought

doctrine's renewed discussion, which became important in the composition of the Reinsdorf Theses that opposed the universality of the church (1933), and then again in the Ansbach Reply, which repudiated the Barmen Declaration (1934) of the Confessing Church.[27]

Historian Richard V. Pierard notes that due to the massive amount of literature produced on the topic and the fact that it did not receive a systematic treatment by Luther himself, not to mention its contradictory and vague treatment by the Wittenberg Reformers, the doctrine of the two kingdoms remains an "exercise in interpretation."[28] The Nazi contribution was to separate the domains of private and public life. Hermann Jordan, an early voice in favor of separation, argued that "the independence of political life from faith is the fruit of Luther's distinction between the two kingdoms."[29]

An example of the influence of this separation became enmeshed with the curriculum in Germany schools. Only one year following Hitler's coming to power, the following passage was being learnt and recited:

> As Jesus set men free from sin and hell, so Hitler rescued the German people from destruction. Both Jesus and Hitler were persecuted; but, while Jesus was crucified, Hitler was exalted to Chancellor. While the disciples of Jesus betrayed their master and left him in his distress, the sixteen friends of Hitler stood by him. The apostles completed the work of their Lord. We hope that Hitler will lead his work to completion. Jesus built for heaven; Hitler, for the German soil.[30]

Bonhoeffer himself appeared to accept the separation between church and government on a foundational level, but made the important distinction, unlike the interpretation of Reich

---

27. Wright, *Martin Luther's Understanding of God's Two Kingdoms*, 32; see also Pierard, "Lutheran Two-Kingdoms Doctrine," 201. For a reproduction of the Ansbach Reply, see Hetzer, *Deutsche Stunde*, 257–59.

28. Pierard, "Lutheran Two-Kingdoms Doctrine," 193–94.

29. Ibid., 198.

30. Robertson, *The Shame and Sacrifice*, 88–89.

thinkers, that the purpose of the government was not a discussion in which the church was prohibited to trespass.[31] It was on this issue, raised in the context of the fair treatment of the Jews, that Bonhoeffer's turn to a more secular posturing of church activity marked the direction of his later theology in which secular life should and must be interpreted theologically, an idea that would take its most poignant form in his *Ethics*.[32]

The importance of Luther's doctrine here is not Bonhoeffer's initial response to it but the way in which he later thinks through it to reject the particular Reich interpretation as being a false dichotomy. Indeed, Luther's doctrine does not lead to a God whose left hand does not know what his right is doing but as Christ who is the ground of all reality. Kelly notes that for Bonhoeffer, "Luther wanted . . . to bring about a better secularity in a Christianity fully attuned to an integration of the spiritual with the secular."[33] While there is no talk of *perichoresis* (since Bonhoeffer is more interested in the church's ability to check the state), and while the kingdoms function on the basis of their operative principles, as Pierard notes, the two kingdoms are not autonomous in the sense that their principles lie outside the dominion of God's judgment.

Søren Kierkegaard

One cannot say precisely how Kierkegaard influences Bonhoeffer since the latter never specifically attributes his thought to the former in a manner that allows point-for-point comparisons.[34] In several of Bonhoeffer's papers from Union Theological Seminary,

---

31. Bonhoeffer scholars have noted that he moves away from the language of orders of creation to orders of preservation in "The Church and the Jewish Question." However, in the same work, Bonhoeffer notes that the church only has indirect access to the government and therefore operates in an advisory role (*DBWE* 12, 2/13).

32. Although prior to *Ethics*, *Discipleship* is in essence a document dedicated to an interpretation of Luther's doctrine, for it attempts to ground faith in a world where it is gradually being extinguished (*DBWE* 4, 8–9).

33. Kelly, "Kierkegaard as 'Antidote,'" 151.

34. Plant, *Bonhoeffer*, 46.

however, Kierkegaard is listed among those whom he recalls with particular reverence. Here, Kierkegaard, who regarded himself standing outside the church, remains for Bonhoeffer one of the pillars upon which the church rests. In his essay "Concerning the Christian Idea of God," Bonhoeffer includes Kierkegaard along with Paul, Augustine, Luther, and Barth as genuine Christian thinkers.[35] In his seminar paper "The Theology of Crisis" from this same period, Bonhoeffer states that "we stand in the tradition of Paul, Luther, Kierkegaard, in the tradition of genuine Christian thinking."[36] A solitary entry in Bonhoeffer's Spanish diary from January–March 1928 mentions his disappointment with the youth in his Spanish choral group who seem unacquainted with the youth movement (*Jugendbewegung*) that swept through Germany during the post-war years. The movement celebrated important cultural authors, and Kierkegaard was among the favorites.[37] Similarly, Kierkegaard's *Augenblick*, an abridged German version of his *Attack upon Christendom*, was suggested by Richard Widmann in November 1925 as research in preparation for Bonhoeffer's work on *Sanctorum Communio*.[38] Perhaps most personal of all is the recommendation Bonhoeffer made to his fiancée while in prison, encouraging her to pick up the Danish philosopher's work. In this way, as Kelly points out, "Kierkegaard's impact on Bonhoeffer lasted throughout his ministry, though with the reservations that eclectic Bonhoeffer had with any and all of his sources."[39]

What can be said summarily about Bonhoeffer and Kierkegaard is that both men are interested in answering the question of ethics as a concern that originates in one's relationship with God. For Kierkegaard, the deconstruction of ethics as the universal powerfully drives home the sense of the individual's solitude in the ethical moment (*Augenblick*).[40] Kierkegaard's contribution to

35. *DBWE* 10, 2/16, 460.
36. Ibid., 2/17, 463.
37. Ibid., 1/5, 63, n. 24.
38. *DBWE* 9, 1/97, 158.
39. Kelly, "Kierkegaard as 'Antidote,'" 145.
40. Gregor, "Bonhoeffer's 'Christian Social Philosophy,'" 206.

Bonhoeffer here is not in the identification of ambiguous ethical situations. Like Bonhoeffer, the *how* is not important; rather what matters is the expression of existential openness.

Stephen Plant writes that what can be drawn out of Kierkegaard's *Fear and Trembling* is an issue that is fundamental to Bonhoeffer's ethics as a whole: the "teleological suspension of the ethical."[41] The concept draws out the insufficiencies of ethical principles against the primacy of faith, the conflict of which is brought to life through the story of Abraham and Isaac. Unique to Kierkegaard is that this story is divided into multiple accounts, each told from a different perspective. In each case, it is a midrashic hermeneutic that projects thoughts, feelings, and situations into the narrative that are absent from the Biblical account. This is done in an effort to demonstrate the insufficiency of the ethical command that prohibits Abraham from killing his son against the more important divine command to obedience. The move itself is directed against the predominance of Kantian and Hegelian thinking, which held ethics to be universal. Immanuel Kant, defender of the "moral law within," calls the voice of God in this "myth" into question.

> For if God should really speak to man, man could still never know that it was God speaking. It is quite impossible for man to apprehend the infinite by his senses, distinguish it from sensible beings, and recognize it as such. But in some cases man can be sure that the voice he hears is not God's; for if the voice commands him to do something contrary to the moral law, then no matter how majestic the apparition may be, and no matter how it may seem to surpass the whole of nature, he must consider it an illusion.[42]

---

41. Plant, *Bonhoeffer*, 46–47; I would note also that unlike James Deotis Roberts, who sees Bonhoeffer's appropriation of this concept as an exception to the rule of pacifism, the genuine thrust of this parallel is in Bonhoeffer's total rejection of deontology and universally sustainable principles of moral behavior, which itself must include pacifism *per se* (see *Bonhoeffer and King*, 107).

42. Kant, *Conflict of the Faculties*, 115.

Influences in Bonhoeffer's Ethical Thought

Likewise, G. W. F. Hegel, who shared no fondness for Abraham, writes, "The first act which made Abraham the progenitor of a nation is a disseverance [Trennung] which snaps the bonds of communal life and love."[43] For Hegel, the fact that Abraham could follow a strange voice was an abandonment of his people and the very order of nature given by God. The father of faith was a suspicious usurper. Kierkegaard's intellectual interest in the story of Abraham counters the enormous significance placed on reason by European thinkers by raising the profile of faith beyond the realm of feeling.[44]

This suspension of the ethical is worked out through a postscript analysis known as *Problema I*. Here Kierkegaard assembles the problem. The ethical is the universal. It is at all times beyond the individual and is not undone by the critical moment. Traditional thinking supposes that when the individual is in temptation or sins, he has violated the ethical by selfishly placing his own interests ahead of the universal. The problem for Kierkegaard is the solution. If the interests of an individual must always be those of the ethical, then the ethical effaces the individual and his or her individuality before God. God is therefore not in relationship with the individual but with a catalog of rules that must be kept. Furthermore the line between the individual and the ethical is essentially blurred. If the goal of the individual is the same as the ethical, there can be no true statement of its power over the individual.

Kierkegaard surmised that the ethical must remain a principle itself and not be dependent upon the individual. If this was to be the case, however, then the individual must experience something altogether different from the principle, i.e., the ethical outside the structural tyranny of the universal. It is only with regard to faith that one is said to be in sin or in grace, and Kierkegaard shifts attention from violation of the commandment to rending of a relationship. Kierkegaard does not undo the commandments, but he implies that sin and grace are not the proper subject matter of the commandments. Nevertheless, as Charles Guignon and

---

43. Hegel, *Early Theological Writings*, 185.
44. Carlisle, *Kierkegaard: A Guide for the Perplexed*, 111.

Derk Pereboom note, "Having faith is not like being an outlaw who rejects ethical principles altogether. If Abraham's faith did away with the ethical, there would be no need for him to struggle with God's command."[45] This is a struggle that Bonhoeffer himself will personally discover through his own ethic against the pressures of Decalogue commandment-based living.

A consequence of Abraham's individuality, which cannot sufficiently answer the ethical, requires that he, Abraham, must stand alone in faith before God. That faith may very well look like sin and sin like faith cannot be avoided, especially for Abraham, who in performing the commandment is guilty of murder. This was a paradox that Bonhoeffer would ultimately take upon himself: faith is one's orientation to ethical being even where the ethical fails to affirm this relationship. Faith is not simply *response*, for this would require that one sets himself up under an ethical rubric where faith becomes the measure of one's ability to sustain personal commitment to an impersonal commandment. Bonhoeffer's understanding of faith is proper to the ethical sphere of humanity's being before God—a sphere that is at first relational, in which openness is more precious than commitment, that acknowledges by taking into itself ethical being, rather than being marginalized to a supporting role. Kierkegaard must have taken on significant meaning to Bonhoeffer as he saw the Confessing Church failing to be the community of Christ.

Kelly notes that Heinrich Traugott Vogel in his study *Christus als Vorbild und Versöhner: Eine kritische Studie zum Problem des Verhältnisses von Gesetz und Evangelium im Werke Sören Kierkegaards* (1968) pointed out that the concept of costly and cheap grace were connected to Kierkegaard's own work *Der Einzelne und die Kirche. Über Luther und den Protestantismus*.[46] The concept of grace is a critical component of Bonhoeffer's analysis of true discipleship, and authenticates the individual's existence in a meaningful relationship with Christ, as opposed to one of

---

45. Guignon and Pereboom, *Existentialism*, 17.
46. Kelly, "Kierkegaard as 'Antidote,'" 149.

formal distinction. True ethics for Bonhoeffer is always a matter of relationship. Kierkegaard's analysis, however, is not without its problems for Bonhoeffer. One difficulty that arises comes in Kierkegaard's notion that the "individual is higher than the ethical." By this Kierkegaard seeks to express the individual in isolation and apart from any intervening influences save his faith in God. Bonhoeffer can at least agree that "Christ makes everyone he calls into an individual. Each is called alone. Each must follow alone."[47] Nonetheless, isolation for Bonhoeffer never means one is entirely apart from the community, because it is always in the community where the individual must locate himself, a community which is both the historical and transcendent body of Christ. Kelly, too, writes that "For Bonhoeffer, Kierkegaard's radical subjectivism lacks the give and take of relationships that impact directly and indirectly on the origins of personhood. Hence, he writes that he departs from Kierkegaard who has insisted that 'becoming a person is an act of the self-establishing I—to be sure in a state of ethical decision.'"[48] In *Creation and Fall*, Bonhoeffer explains that freedom is not freedom for one's self, but freedom for others. "Freedom is a relationship between two persons. Being free means 'being-free-for-the-other,' because I am bound to the other. Only by being in relation with the other am I free."[49] To be outside the community is to deny God, for Christ meets us in the other individual. As Luca Bagetto writes, "In the community the appeal is admittedly *ad personam*, but it is marked as well by a trans-individual and historical aspect. Revelation does not manifest itself only in the instant of evidence and in the punctuality of the individual's decision, but unfolds itself in the historical continuity of the community."[50] This is apparent in Bonhoeffer's analysis of the *Kollectivperson* (see chapter 4), in which he develops the idea that individual sin is the bearing of one's sins

---

47. *DBWE* 4, 92.
48. Kelly, "Kierkegaard as 'Antidote,'" 159.
49. *DBWE* 3, 63.
50. Bagetto, "The Exemplification of Decision," 197.

as humanity; so, too, the individual is authorized to speak for the church because of its trans-individual character.

A second problem is that Kierkegaard's context for the problem of ethics is largely a psychologically probing casuistry that is told through a story of remarkable narrative. God does not address the average person under such circumstances, expecting that person to draw out of the seeming confusion a new appreciation that the new demand places on the individual, and one which supersedes the universal that all his life he has held precisely to be the revelation of God. Like Bonhoeffer, humans are typically devoid of such divine intervention. For Kierkegaard, whether or not God speaks is not the point. This is because God's speaking is not an event deferred to the judgment of the community. The community, for Kierkegaard, is largely apostate, wanting only what Roger L. Shinn writes, "the conventional, comfortable life . . . instead of for lonely, courageous obedience to Christ."[51] It is rather what the individual does in his aloneness that matters, meaning that how a person hears God is not as important as what he or she does with what is heard. Walter Kaufmann indeed has memorably criticized Kierkegaard on the position of private faith as being a dangerous principle of action.[52]

Perhaps the greatest rift that emerges between Bonhoeffer and Kierkegaard picks up on this former point and is with regard to the former's emphasis on the community of saints. Although Bonhoeffer could appreciate the personal sobriety required of Kierkegaard's ethical isolation before God, a feeling that must have been bitter during his years in the Confessing Church as he watched friends acquiesce and their support dwindle, he recognized that there was simply no such isolation afforded to the Christian who acts with the community in mind. As Rasmussen writes, "Immersion in the life of the community of the saints, the Body of Christ, and theological insight are the indispensable starting points."[53]

---

51. Shinn, *The Existentialist Posture: A Christian Look at its Meaning, Impact, Values, and Dangers*, 54.

52. Kaufmann, *From Shakespeare to Existentialism*, 178.

53. Rasmussen, *Dietrich Bonhoeffer: Reality and Resistance*, 24.

INFLUENCES IN BONHOEFFER'S ETHICAL THOUGHT

Friedrich Nietzsche

At first glance, Nietzsche does not appear a likely candidate in the formation of a theologian. His attacks on the church and Christianity are infamous, written with incendiary passion, which, for better or worse, have helped to frame his legacy among his readers. Some of his most biting vitriol comes in *The Anti-Christ*, a work that misses no opportunity to impugn the foundations of the Christian faith. Here, as in other places, Nietzsche claims to uncover the disastrous origins of Christian ethics and its consequences for the human spirit. As Frits De Lange writes, "In Nietzsche's eyes, the two thousand years of Christian culture represents the biggest moral injury ever committed in the history of humankind."[54]

One hears in Nietzsche the faint echoes of ancient critics, of Pyrrhonian skepticism, and of Christianity's early critics; of Celsus and Epictetus, who decried the contrast between the herd mentality of the practicing laity.[55] One hears a communal critique in Nietzsche's distaste for the "first Christians" and the "inescapable corruption within the first congregation."[56] It was these first congregations, which expanded into the "cruder masses of people," who failed to capture the free-spirited message of their Christ and the "original symbolism" of the cross, which in turn vulgarized Christianity, making it "barbaric."[57] Subsequently, even those alleged to enjoy close kinship to Christ are impugned. There is no love lost for the apostle Paul, whom Nietzsche describes as an "insolent windbag."[58] For Nietzsche, Christianity is one continuing error of misdirection. Conversely, Christ avoided the *ressentiment* that is intrinsic in his followers; "his image had not had any

---

54. De Lange, "Aristocratic Christendom," 73.
55. See Nietzsche, *Twilight of the Idols*, § 1. Nietzsche also disdained the cult of Christian martyrdom (cf. Nietzsche, *The Anti-Christ*, § 53), which was berated by critics like Celsus and the Stoics Epictetus, Seneca, and Aurelius for the ignoble way in which Christians sought to destroy themselves.
56. Nietzsche, *The Anti-Christ*, § 44.
57. Ibid., § 37.
58. Ibid., § 46.

15

belligerent, no-saying, no-doing features at all"[59]—in essence, the heart of the Christian morality.

Nietzsche was not merely attacking a historical manifestation of Christianity in which the hypocrisy of believers created a world of contradiction. Nietzsche was attempting to raze Christianity at its foundations precisely because Christ was not that foundation. For, in his eyes, there had only been one Christian, and he died on the cross.[60]

Christian ethics remained a broad target, which Nietzsche supported with *ad hoc*, but otherwise effective, examples taken both from the tradition and German culture. In Nietzsche's view, Christian ethics taught life-negating value. It prized weakness over strength. It enslaved rather than freed. And it rejoiced in making the world ugly.

But not all readers of Nietzsche agree that he was toxic to the Christian witness. Nietzsche proved to be a much-needed critic in Germany. If he had an axe to grind, that same axe could be used for the job of testing an armor that had softened with age and inveteracy. And theologians recognized the value in this. As Craig Wiley writes, "Among religious thinkers, Nietzsche is neither unquestioningly accepted nor rejected; he is wrestled with and analyzed, co-opted and contradicted. Even Christians, for whom he reserved special bile, have found Nietzsche's writings useful."[61] That these thinkers took Nietzsche seriously in Germany is evidenced by the fact that Nietzsche even crossed over to the pulpit, a phenomenon that puzzled Bonhoeffer.[62] Yet what did not puzzle Bonhoeffer was Nietzsche's importance to the theological task.

For Bonhoeffer, Nietzsche's influence took root early. One of Bonhoeffer's teachers at the Grunewald Gymnasium was Martin

---

59. Ibid., § 38.
60. Ibid., § 39.
61. Wiley, "I was Dead and Behold," 508.
62. In an essay on how to select a text for preaching (1930), Bonhoeffer writes, "the Bible is God's Word . . . and a religious poem by Nietzsche is not." (*DBWE* 10, 2/5, 382–83). Ironically, Bonhoeffer himself is guilty of using Nietzsche in support of his own work (for example, in his own sermon on 1 John 2:17 on August 26, 1928 (3/10, 517).

Influences in Bonhoeffer's Ethical Thought

Havenstein who wrote on Nietzsche. Peter Frick notes that "it seems conceivable . . . to surmise that a teacher who is absorbed in the thought of Nietzsche to the extent that he wrote a work on the philosopher would share some of his insights with his students."[63] That the philosopher had a lasting effect on Bonhoeffer is significant as late as his writing of *Ethics*. Rades writes that "Nietzsche is mentioned more often than any other theologian and philosopher apart from Kant and Luther."[64] De Lange makes the claim that Bonhoeffer was drawn to Nietzsche by a strength of character cultivated in the former's home, which helped him to recognize the same in Nietzsche's philosophy. This translated into Bonhoeffer's impatience and contempt for fellow prisoners at Tegel. While Bonhoeffer at times did assert himself against those who were not action-oriented, such behavior fails as a principle of uniform interpretation and is at odds with what we know about other accounts from Tegel. Recollections of Bonhoeffer during this period that appear regularly in the literature hardly depict a callous or even unbreakable individual. On the contrary, Bonhoeffer is remembered for his kind treatment of fellow prisoners. Furthermore, his strength of character was tested as time wore on. He suffered from depression, calling himself in an autobiographical poem written at this time in Tegel,[65] "restless and longing, and sick / like a bird in a cage / Struggling for breath . . ." He pined for his former life and fiancée, and even mentioned grapplings with suicide (whether he was suicidal or not is debatable). One might safely argue that conflicts such as these are not congruent with the kind of *Übermensch* that Nietzsche sought to cultivate.[66] Leaving aside the argument deriving from strength of character, which nevertheless is not entirely convincing, there is

---

63. Frick, "Friedrich Nietzsche's Aphorisms and Dietrich Bonhoeffer's Theology," 175.

64. Rades, "Nietzsche and Bonhoeffer," 4.

65. "Who am I?" *DBWE* 8, 3/173, 459–60.

66. Bethge reports that Bonhoeffer's suicidal tendencies were at best temptations and only had the effect of burdening, rather than undoing, him. (*Dietrich Bonhoeffer: A Biography*, 832–33).

enough evidence in Bonhoeffer's writing to confine oneself to identifying Nietzsche's influence. It is to this we will turn.

Bonhoeffer not only set out to answer Nietzsche, but adopted elements of his approach. Reinhart Staats writes, "It is similarly striking how Bonhoeffer provides a surprising Christian interpretation to the call of the European philosopher Friedrich Nietzsche not only, as already seen, regarding loyalty to the earth but also in the commandment "to love those farthest away."[67] Nietzsche's influence on Bonhoeffer's ethics has been analyzed in various ways, including assertions in Giles Fraser's notion of Christian salvation through freedom and de Lange's comparison of the two thinkers in the context of salt-of-the-earth worldly living.[68]

Nietzsche's own approach to ethics is summarized succinctly by Simon May. "What always determines whether Nietzsche approves of a particular value in a particular context is, first, the manner in which it is reached—i.e. whether it is reached by the sovereign choice of the noble type or whether by the reactive 'universalism' of the moral type—and, second, what purposes it serves—i.e. whether to enhance life and individuality ('ascending life'), or whether to deny life and individuality ('descending life')."[69] With regard to these criteria, Nietzsche's disapproval of Christianity comes first in what he sees as the manipulation of idealism. "In the world of Christian representations, nothing that happens has any bearing on reality: on the contrary, we have recognized the instinct of hatred against every reality as the driving, only driving element, at the root of Christianity."[70] Bonhoeffer is well aware of this problem.[71] Nietzsche asks, "Is the 'terrible' truth not that

---

67. *DBWE* 10, 630.

68. Fraser writes, "Nietzsche and Bonhoeffer conceive of 'salvation' as some sort of reversal of the original 'moral' fall: both envisage salvation as looking something like the sort of life led by Adam and Eve before the fall." *Redeeming Nietzsche*, 5 (cf. de Lange, "Aristocratic Christendom," 77).

69. May, *Nietzsche's Ethics*, 53.

70. Nietzsche, *The Anti-Christ*, § 39.

71. De Lange observes Bonhoeffer's use of the word *Hinterweltler* (a term coined by Nietzsche) in relation to an idealistic world existing alongside the material world Christians should inhabit. "Aristocratic Christendom," 79.

no amount of knowledge about an act ever suffices to ensure its performance, that the space between knowledge and action has never yet been bridged even in once single instance?"[72] Nietzsche observes that the German nobility continues to parrot a system of ethics even as they themselves ignore its practice, which for this very reason indicts the justification of Christianity for its impossible idealism and makes its handlers hypocrites. With the repudiation of idealism, Nietzsche wants to challenge the Christian monopoly on morality,[73] claiming that the idealism pronounced in the morals of Christian living is borne out of a slave mentality in which the weak wish to control the strong. Nietzsche, son of a Lutheran minister, recognizes that negotiating a path between good and evil was never the message of Christ.[74]

Even while Bonhoeffer recognizes the problem, he is not ready to concede all to Nietzsche. Bethge reminds us that "Bonhoeffer could not let Nietzsche have a monopoly of loyalty to the earth."[75] So Bonhoeffer writes, "The discovery of what is beyond good and evil was not made by Friedrich Nietzsche, who from this standpoint utters polemics against the hypocrisy of Christianity; it belongs to the original material of the Christian message, concealed, of course, as it is ... The Christian message stands beyond good and evil."[76]

Nietzsche is not at all ignorant to the ethical form of Christ. In an enlightening passage, he writes, "Jesus said to his Jews: The

72. Nietzsche, *Daybreak*, Bk 2, § 116.
73. Nietzsche, *Ecce Homo*, § 6 and 7.
74. Nietzsche, *The Anti-Christ*, § 39.
75. Weissbach, "Christology and Ethics," 99.
76. Tödt notes that with respect to Bonhoeffer's methodological criteria of overcoming the disunion (*Entzweiung*) of good and evil, Bonhoeffer's statement from 1942 is consistent with his concern in Barcelona (1928–1929), namely that "the knowledge of good and evil appears to be the goal of all ethical reflection. The first task of Christian ethics is to do away with that knowledge" ("Authentic Faith," 122, n. 31). It is worth noting that Nietzsche, the son of a Lutheran pastor, was not naive enough to believe Christ was only a moral lawgiver. Thus, he writes on Christ: "This bearer of 'glad tidings' died the way he lived, the way he taught—not 'to redeem humanity,' but instead to demonstrate how people need to live" (*The Anti-Christ*, § 35).

law was for servants—love God as I do, as his son! Why should we care about morals, we sons of God?"[77]

This slave morality in Nietzsche, a morality that deprives one of his or her vitality, becomes for Bonhoeffer the distance between freedom and the inauthentic life. Bonhoeffer never formally adopts the existentially charged term "inauthenticity" in the same way it is attributed to Heidegger, primarily because inauthenticity in Heidegger is something from which the individual disentangles. It is enough for Bonhoeffer to understand inauthenticity as an inappropriate evaluation of the division between being and reflection, which occurs when the individual fails to accept that he occupies both of these dimensions simultaneously.[78] And so Bonhoeffer, reflecting on Nietzsche's conception of Christian morality, ponders, "What is the meaning of weakness in this world? We know that Christianity has been blamed ever since its early days for its message to the weak. Christianity is a religion of slaves, of people with inferiority complexes; it owes its success only to the masses of miserable people."[79]

Bonhoeffer believes Nietzsche's indictment of Christianity is wrong precisely because his criticism is pointed at an *epigone*. For Bonhoeffer, the true church is birthed in freedom. And freedom is the life that goes beyond good and evil to find Christ as its goal, so that through Christ one is released from existential slavery. The Nietzsche who celebrated the life-affirming *Übermensch* is met in the God of Bonhoeffer who is not the facilitator of human weakness but who is directly in the fray with us. And so Bonhoeffer writes that God is "not on the boundaries but at the center, not in weakness but in strength; and therefore not in death and guilt but in man's life and good."[80]

---

77. Nietzsche, *Beyond Good and Evil*, § 164.

78. For more, see *DBWE* 6, 247 (cf. *DBWE* 2, 70/a).

79. Frick notes in Bonhoeffer's sermon on 2 Corinthians 12:9 in London that "whereas Nietzsche proclaimed the reevaluation of all values as a feat of the overman, Bonhoeffer assigns the creation of values exclusively to Christ." Frick, "Friedrich Nietzsche's Aphorisms and Dietrich Bonhoeffer's Theology," 182.

80. *DBWE* 8, 3/137, 366–67.

In this way Bonhoeffer is not disagreeing with Nietzsche's Christ, who also is beyond good and evil, but is taking issue with his critical treatment of the church, which Nietzsche believes manipulated the life message of its founder as an act of self-preservation.

The irony of this statement should not be ignored when one considers that Bonhoeffer himself discovered what it meant to go from a fairly aristocratic upbringing, where he was able to write and intellectualize freely all the while traveling the world at his father's expense, to the prison cell, the brink of despair, and personal surrender. In experiencing these two sides of life, Bonhoeffer could not simply read the call of Christ to be a marching order for the weak to join the strong. This call had to be reinterpreted. Bonhoeffer recognized that of those who survive the worst of circumstances, the weak are indeed the strong when their strength is encouraged through God, not as a boundary condition encountered with their eyes towards heaven but in the immediate crisis that comes in living faithfully to God through one's trials.

In his last days, Bonhoeffer could track with Nietzsche. The Nietzsche who ponders in his aphorisms whether we would see the last of religion finds its parallel in Bonhoeffer who spoke of the coming religionless Christianity in a late letter from prison. This observation included the reevaluation of a new language for speaking about the common Christian experience.[81]

Reinhold Seeberg

If Kierkegaard was for Bonhoeffer the influence who challenged the idea of the ethical as a transcendent reality superior to the individual, then it was Reinhold Seeberg who stirred Bonhoeffer to consider how transcendence is grasped within the community.

---

81. Nietzsche, *The Gay Science*, § 108: "After Buddha was dead, they still showed his shadow in a cave for centuries —a tremendous, gruesome shadow. God is dead; but given the way people are, there may still for millennia be caves in which they show his shadow—And we—we must still defeat his shadow as well!" See also Bonhoeffer's letter to Bethge on April 30, 1944 (*DBWE* 8, 3/137, 361–67).

Rumscheidt remarks that up to the time of Bonhoeffer's *Habilitationsschrift*, Seeberg is mentioned 134 times; and that his dissertation is littered with references to Seeberg's *Christiche Dogmatik*.[82] This should be no surprise since Seeberg became Bonhoeffer's advisor during the writing of *Sanctorum Communio*. The fact that Bonhoeffer chose Seeberg, a professor of systematic theology and social ethics at Berlin, as his advisor over the eminent Adolf von Harnack, one of the greatest theologians in his day, suggests the respect claimed by Seeberg in German theology.[83] Seeberg's influence on Bonhoeffer's engagement with ethics seems apparent from a letter on October 19, 1928, in which Seeberg encourages Bonhoeffer to pursue either the ethical problems from the twelfth century through the work of John of Salisbury or a history of ethical dogma on the Sermon on the Mount.[84] Furthermore, when Bonhoeffer was first asked to preach on ethics in Barcelona, he drew from the wells he was currently digging in conversations with Seeberg, and so took the opportunity to apply these theological exchanges to his sermons.

Seeberg's own theological program is best described in his commitment to "positive theology" by way of voluntarism. As Tödt writes, this theme carries throughout Bonhoeffer's entire career.[85] Seeberg casts the problem of German theology, with regard to its subservience to transcendentalism and epistemology, and imagines in his own writing the social dimension of participating in Christ.[86] As Rumscheidt notes, "the form of our participation in [religious knowledge] is the application of Christian morality to concrete so-

---

82. Rumscheidt, "Significance of Adolf von Harnack," 201. The *Habilitationsschrift* was a thesis written and researched at the post-doctorate level that qualified the candidate to teach in the German university.

83. See Bonhoeffer's letter in *DBWE* 9, 1/93, 148.

84. *NRS*, 36.

85. Gerald Birney Smith, writing at the time of the new approach, notes the significance of the term, in that "positive is intended to mark off this type of theology from the extreme liberalism which comes to 'negative' conclusions concerning many of the central doctrines of Christianity" ("Modern-Positive Movement," 94–95; see also Tödt, *Authentic Faith*, 79–80).

86. Rumscheidt, "Significance of Adolf von Harnack," 204.

cial, political, and national problems."⁸⁷ When Bonhoeffer articulates his concept of the *Kollectivperson*, he is likely being influenced by Seeberg who "appealed to the will of humans both qua individuals and qua members of corporate communal entities."⁸⁸ All of this draws on Seeberg's impulse that God's primary mode is will. The contemplative component of God's self-reflection is unintelligible and is sacrificed for raw action. Action is the sociological mode of the church. When God's will depends upon his reason, action is subjugated to contemplation. This has the negative connotation of suggesting that God must weigh an issue before its execution. Contemplation, too, bears the mark of an abstract reality in which action itself is something God must access by reason. In this way, it approximates the scholastic view of the *simplicitas Dei* because the reliance of attributes suggests a composite reality to God's being. For Seeberg, this problem is solved by combining will and intellect, which are at once both located in God's positive action. Although this was true for Seeberg, an explicative treatment of the divine attributes with regard to Bonhoeffer's analysis of the sociality of the church is not essential. Bonhoeffer in fact prefers to draw on the concrete reality of the attributes manifestly understood in the world. I assert that on this point, Bonhoeffer's social realism and lifelong regard for contextualism keep him at arm's length from the scholastic tradition. In this way, he tracks more with Brunner than Aquinas, Anselm, or even Augustine.⁸⁹

This point can also be supported with regard to Bonhoeffer's understanding of transcendence in the ethical, an idea he develops through Seeberg even where he rejects the way in which Seeberg himself develops the concept.⁹⁰

87. Ibid., 203.
88. Ibid.
89. Emil Brunner's criticism is as follows: "This idea of the '*simplicitas Dei*' is inevitable if we make the abstract idea of the Absolute the starting-point for our thought. This is simply the undifferentiated Monas of Neo-Platonism modified by Theism" (*Dogmatics*, Vol. 1, 293).
90. Bonhoeffer does not believe Seeberg has disentangled himself from the charge of idealism, calling his theory of a prior religion a move from "pure transcendentalism to idealism" (see *DBWE* 2, Part A, 57–58).

The influence of Seeberg's "modern-positive" approach to theology helps Bonhoeffer articulate a theology that had practical application in an attempt to take seriously the church as an institution of social consequence.

Seeberg's interest in the interaction between revelation and history also left an impression on Bonhoeffer. Two important instances confirm that this view was entertained as a topic of interest by Bonhoeffer. In his Spanish diary from Barcelona, Bonhoeffer refers to his final meeting with his German youth group on January 18 as a "'moving session' in which the questions of Christianity, history, and religion were raised."[91] In a letter to Seeberg from Barcelona on July 20, 1928, he informs his mentor how he longs to "take a seat once again among your audience and reflect with you on the 'meaning of history.'"[92]

An important consequence of Seeberg's voluntarism for Bonhoeffer is the way the latter extends moral action to concrete, social phenomenon that resists epistemological abstraction and replaces epistemology with what Rumscheidt calls "life-related and experience-focused" events.[93] Between 1901 and 1902, Seeberg delivered sixteen lectures on his view of the Christian faith at the University of Berlin. Among other things, Seeberg expressed the view that moral action can never be judged apart from the person, because it is the will of the person and not the action that determines moral value. Addressing the composition of sin, he writes:

> What really makes them action and gives them moral character is something different. It is inward separation from God, aversion to what is good, unbelief and lovelessness. But that the connection of circumstances and the intensification or limitation of incentives and impulses can allow both outwardly honourable and also

---

91. Ibid., A, 59.

92. *DBWE* 10, 1/36, 119. See also 1/44a, 136, with regard to Bonhoeffer's critique of Brunner's notion of history.

93. Rumschiedt, "Significance of Adolf von Harnack," 203.

criminal activities to proceed from this state of the soul is of course quite intelligible.[94]

It is worth noting that here Seeberg is emphasizing that content is not a measure of worth. The same circumstances that produce the appearance of morally abhorrent actions produce commendable actions as well, a theme that continues throughout Bonhoeffer's ethical thought. Only in the individual can there be a legitimate means to establish the true value of an action. Seeberg makes this point clear in his analysis of the will and moral character.

> One who, in his sphere of life, with its manifold relations, experiences the all-operative God and serves His Kingdom, and who wills and seeks this constantly and with all his strength, is perfect in this seeking and striving. He realises the ideal of the Christian life. One who knows what he wills and wills what he knows is a moral character. The ideal of his life is his firm possession, and he himself has become a conscious organ of this ideal. One who consciously subjects and wills to subject himself to it in faith and love is a Christian character. The Christian character is the Christian life-ideal. The Christian character is the highest form of a moral personality.[95]

One's will is not oriented by individual acts but is qualified by acting out of faith and love through an experience with God. One senses in this the traditional concern about the right response to God, which is a concern that dates back to debates between Luther and Agricola. It is clear that Seeberg is sympathetic to Agricola. Seeberg's concern that law had become an abstraction that deprives the participant of his act of faith can be demonstrated in the following statement: "That is what Christ proclaimed: God is for us, therefore all things serve us; and we are for God, therefore we serve all. And this is the task He lays upon us, not as a law or a theoretical doctrine, but as a gift which we experience, feel, and have in the coming of God's sovereignty over us."[96]

---

94. Seeberg, *Fundamental Truths*, 170–71.
95. Ibid., 323–24.
96. Ibid., 244.

One also sees Seeberg in Bonhoeffer's exposition of original sin. In his *Creation and Fall: A Theological Exposition of Genesis 1–3*, Bonhoeffer argues that sin is not an inherited disease but is an act.[97]

Bonhoeffer's most able attempt at engaging Seeberg is found in *Act and Being*. The work is riddled with Seebergian clues throughout, prompting Wilhelm Lütgert in his review to assert "it cannot be denied that the author is a student of Reinhold Seeberg."[98] Nevertheless, Lütgert notes certain departures from Seeberg. One such departure is an important section on Seeberg that is found in a discussion on the nature of faith. Here Bonhoeffer recalls Seeberg's positive statement on the nature of religion, which he regards as a "mold" into which revelation from God is deposited. While Bonhoeffer has been portrayed as being critical of Seeberg on this point, he holds that his former mentor understands the priority of God's action toward the sinner and includes this in a footnote, referring to Seeberg's *Christliche Dogmatik*.[99]

Bethge offers no details of the break between Seeberg and Bonhoeffer except to note that it was in 1935, a year significant because the Nuremburg laws were introduced. This break, however, seems much less an intellectual than an ideological one. Seeberg's emphasis on community eventually leads him into nationalism. While it has been suggested that Seeberg influenced Bonhoeffer ideologically, in particular regarding certain nationalistic statements Bonhoeffer is supposed to have made during his Barcelona years, it is presumptuous to assume that Bonhoeffer's ideology

97. *DBWE* 3, 150.

98. *DBWE* 10, 1/109a, 210–11.

99. Seeberg writes: "*Von Gott kommt also der Glaube, durch seinen Geist im Wort wird er gewirkt. Dies allgemeine Urteil muß nun aber an der Entstehung des Glaubens geprüft werden, um für seine Art den entsprechenden wissenschaftlichen Ausdruck zu finden . . . Glauben ist in ihnen noch nicht vorhanden, da dar Widerwille gegen den göttlichen Willen nich überwunden ist . . . Für ihn war das Wort nur ein Gefüge von Begriffen. Diese Begriffe fassen sich jetzt zu einer lebendigen Einheit zusammen als ein Wille, der sich auf das menschliche Subjekt richtet, und zwar um seinen Willen zu einer neuen Richtungnahme zu bestimmen, die an die Stelle des bisherigen Widerwillens gegen Gott tritt*" (*Christliche Dogmatik*, Vol. 2, 506–507).

derives from his theological compatibilities with Seeberg found in the context of an academic relationship. Robert Ericksen echoes this claim by arguing against grouping Nazi-era theologians as ideological partners, despite their agreement on basic terms of the Christian faith, since they both supported and resisted Hitler.[100]

Karl Barth

Barth is traditionally recognized as being one of Bonhoeffer's strongest influences. Bonhoeffer was captivated by the great Swiss theologian, and Bethge notes that with "his discovery of dialectical theology, a new certainty replaced Bonhoeffer's restless wanderings. It was a liberation."[101] It was Barth with whom Bonhoeffer longed to visit, and a meeting was made possible by his friend Erwin Sutz. Bonhoeffer struck up a friendship with Barth and was even able to share with him thoughts on ethics, which can be detected in Bonhoeffer's lectures from that time.

That Bonhoeffer and Barth did not always agree is apparent. During their informal discussions on ethics, Barth was concerned that Bonhoeffer had turned grace into a principle upon which all ethics must be done, to the exclusion of other "relative ethical criteria."[102] Nevertheless, one of Barth's most enduring contributions to the shape of Bonhoeffer's ethics remains in what Rasmussen refers to as "ethics as command." "Where Bonhoeffer makes the most of ethics as command he is actually borrowing from Barth

---

100. Ericksen, *Theologians Under Hitler*, 25. One might consider Bonhoeffer's feelings toward Paul Althaus's *Communio Sanctorum* in preparation of his own work of the same title. Godsey writes that "Bonhoeffer expresses his regret that he could use it only sparingly but expresses delight in its support of his own views." ("Doctrine of Love," 191). Althaus, of course, becomes a derisive figure and one of the leading theologians supporting Nazi ideology.

101. Bethge, *Dietrich Bonhoeffer: A Biography*, 74; Barth himself was influenced by Kierkegaard's dialectic, particularly in the concepts of the qualitative dialectic, indirect communication, and paradox. (Oh, *Karl Barth's Trinitarian Theology*, 21.)

102. *NRS*, 116.

and appropriating this for uses of his own."[103] In his article "A Question of Method," Rasmussen points to comparative statements that he believes demonstrate Bonhoeffer's reliance on Barth's material. In June 1981, letters by Bonhoeffer to Barth were discovered. In one of those letters, dated May 13, 1942, Bonhoeffer indicates that he had secured galleys of Barth's *Kirchliche Dogmatik* and he desired to spend some time in solitude reading the second half of the volume. The half to which Bonhoeffer refers, claims Rasmussen, is "The Command of God" in *Church Dogmatics* II/2.[104]

The following points are a sketch of where the two theologians encountered one another conceptually on the ethical view of obedience and command:

1. The command is concrete and not abstract. Barth's and Bonhoeffer's insistence on the substance of the command being the address of God in Jesus Christ ensures that despite the historic person, the question "who Jesus is for us today?" is still relevant. For Bonhoeffer, concretion of the commandment is not history alone; for in saying this we would only focus on the humanity of Christ, thus failing to apprehend his godhead. Rather, concretion is the expression of God's revelation in the doctrine of the incarnation in which the timeless God becomes humanity to affect humanity for all times. The early Barth could also speak about the concrete command in Christ, but for different reasons. As Bethge notes, "[Barth] regarded no historical moment as being *capax infiniti*."[105] This point remains consistent with his Reformed background.

2. The command is definite. It only allows either disobedience or obedience.[106] Obedience is not one's ability at any time to take up a specific action or remain neutral. Any assertion of one's ability to dispatch obedience as one act among many assumes that the command does not come to us as judg-

---

103. Rasmussen. "Question of Method," 115.
104. Ibid., 119–20, n. 59.
105. Bethge, *Dietrich Bonhoeffer: A Biography*, 182.
106. DBWE 4, 77.

Influences in Bonhoeffer's Ethical Thought

ment and its application does not change; it does not require reorientation and self-examination.[107] In this way, Bonhoeffer tracks with Barth with regard to the unavoidability of the moment in which obedience is required. For Barth, however, at this time, while obedience is consigned to its eschatological import, "grace is the power of obedience . . . it is knowledge that requires no act of will to translate it into action."[108] For Bonhoeffer, the problem was sociologically confined to the question of cheap grace that had ravaged the Lutheran landscape, which, according to Haddon Willmer, was akin to "knowing the grace of God," only to "argue ourselves out of obedience."[109] For Bonhoeffer's Luther, true grace and works were inextricably bound in union.

3. With regard to our obedience, the command is permission. This permission frees humanity to obey the command and to live as human beings. So Bonhoeffer writes, "*Gehorsam ohne Freiheit ist Sklaverei, Freiheit ohne Gehorsam ist Willkür.*"[110] The idea that permission frees us to be "human beings" approximates a theme close to Barth in which Jesus Christ represents the real humanity precisely because he is God's "yes" to humanity and affirms this by taking up humanity in himself.[111] Rasmussen has argued that the change from obedience to freedom is the emphasis in *Discipleship* and *Ethics*, respectively.[112] Andreas Pangritz states that this view was adopted from Bonhoeffer's reading of Barth's *Church Dogmatics*.[113] Barth writes, "The form by which the commandment of God is distinguished from all other commands, the special

---

107. Barth, *Church Dogmatics*, 1.2:836.
108. Barth, *Epistle to the Romans*, 207.
109. Willmer, "Costly Discipleship," 176.
110. "Obedience without freedom is slavery, freedom without obedience is arbitrariness" (*DBW* 6:287; see also n. 224).
111. Mikkelsen, *Reconciled Humanity*, 88.
112. Rasmussen, *Dietrich Bonhoeffer: Reality and Resistance*, 50.
113. Pangritz, "Dietrich Bonhoeffer," 273.

form . . . consists in the fact that it is permission—the granting of a very definite freedom."[114]

These commonalities, writes Rasmussen, are "genuine Bonhoeffer, though not original. The themes of concreteness and specificity of the command, the emphasis given obedience, the Christocentricity of the command, the embrace of all of life by the command and the conferring of freedom—all these have genuine and strong antecedents pre-dating Bonhoeffer's study of Church Dogmatics II/2." Nevertheless, it is "Bonhoeffer as the student of Barth."[115]

The significance of these influential thinkers both in the living tradition (as with Barth and Seeberg) and the classic tradition (as with Luther, Kierkegaard, and Nietzsche) helps to clarify Bonhoeffer's own reactions to a rapidly changing cultural and political landscape of his time, and serves as a continual point of balance and intellectual reflection that buffers against the rising tide of ideological domination represented in National Socialism. As a theologian who was attracted to the dialectical thinking of those like Barth and the realization of modernity's inability to solve its own internal crises, as well as the loss of a moral center, Bonhoeffer found himself in an intellectual backlash against rationalism that was being carried out in the larger culture. Awareness of his own intellectual position, and perhaps the Barthian rejection of religious tribalism, made it difficult for Bonhoeffer to align with a Christianity that was being summoned to revitalize the *Volksgemeinschaft* as the visible presence of God's moral authority at the expense of the broader reach of the faith. In Bonhoeffer's theological reflections, one not only sees his own developing thinking on the ethical issues of his day, but a cast of conversation partners who help him define what he gradually saw to be his role in resisting Nazi Socialist rule.

---

114. Barth, *Church Dogmatics*, 2.2:585.
115. Rasmussen, "Question of Method," 124–25.

2

Bonhoeffer's Ethical Method

HAVING LOOKED AT THE ways in which Bonhoeffer was in dialogue with important thinkers in the tradition of continental philosophy and theology, I now turn to examine Bonhoeffer's method used to analyze ethical dilemmas and constructs. By method, I want to emphasize how Bonhoeffer adapts the ethical question prior to any ethical presupposition or consideration of theme or content. Asking the ethical question as a means of methodological approach is not about achieving specific results nor response. In this sense, we avoid certain elements of formal ethical thinking in which the individual is subjugated to pre-existing structures and extensions of a communal ideal. Yet, *method* takes in the ways we think about ethics as both a formal and material construct. A material ethic inhabits our formal language, institutions, and creeds as accepted by the community, but all the while offers itself to us as a lived experienced, insofar as its authority is given with its being. Likewise, the lived experience of being in Christ rejects a solipsistic approach in which no formal structuring of the ethical experience exists. For example, the celebration of the Lord's Supper is an ordinance experienced both in community and individually, as well as formally and materially. Because Bonhoeffer lives within these two options, being that he continues to respect the formal principle and authority of the Church, when we speak of his method we are invariably speaking both of the material ethical reality of Christ and the formal appropriation of an ethical Christology. The free composition of Christ is his affirmation of the individual as well as others ensuring that revelation is a shared experience. The result of this is that we find ourselves already operating within a theological language, both through the tradition of the church and the reality of the world as it is given to us. Although peace may have been Bonhoeffer's "first great theme,"[1] the same is ultimately a filter that must not be construed as methodologically proper.

I will begin this chapter by looking at other ethical approaches and how Bonhoeffer rejects them, which will in course lead to an analysis of his own method.

Deontological Ethics

Deontological approaches to ethics are the most traditional type of method, and the one most commonly appropriated in non-scholarly and lay circles. In deontological ethics, one affirms rules of conduct and principles that are generally valid outside and beyond the reality in which they are functionally expressed. Similarly, commandments are understood as nonnegotiable ordinances from God whose content, while subject to interpretation, is already given prior to any consideration of circumstance. The priority of identifying predictable action associated with the commandment demands that the commandment, and consequently one's duty, rather than the dilemma in which the ethic itself becomes a question, is of primary importance. Bethge recalls Bonhoeffer's rejection of this method of doing ethics in a comment during the time of Bonhoeffer's imprisonment and interrogation: "The logical consequences of his actions, unusual for a Lutheran pastor and theologian, will appear more plainly than ever in the latter account of the interrogations, and may shock the susceptibilities of anyone whose standards are those of traditional ethics and normal times. But one has to realize that what went on in those interrogations

---

1. "Peace," says Bethge in an interview, was Bonhoeffer's "first great theme for his young life. Being a Christian means to work for peace." Boehlke and Drake, *Dietrich Bonhoeffer: Memories and Perspectives*.

was only a continuation of what had been thought out and decided long before."[2]

Subterfuge, lying, and hiding the identities of the conspirators—all such things would be difficult to justify in a classic deontological ethical approach. Bonhoeffer expresses the weakness of deontological ethics in the following statement, which is only one of many of its kind: "The possibility of judging whether our action is good lies alone in Christ, the present and future One. All other 'secure' possibilities, which appear to give continuity to the action, are to be rejected."[3] Bonhoeffer then proceeds to enumerate such concepts.

The failure of deontological ethics in Bonhoeffer's estimation lies in its potential for abstraction, for which the practical consequence is a tendency toward generalization. Stephen Plant translates a question to the Christian project: "Are Christian ethics really unique, in which case Christians are in the world but shaped by values and practices that distinguish them sharply from prevailing social mores, the only proper measure of which is not what impact their way of life has but the extent to which it witnesses faithfully to Christ?"[4] The answer is that no ethical practice can specifically identify a person as being a Christian. And so Bonhoeffer concludes, "The search for a generally valid Christian norm or precept is completely hopeless."[5]

Another reason Bonhoeffer rejected deontological ethics was because history is such a poor indicator of any sustainable principle. What is good in one age is evil in the next. Principles so often ignore the historical form and are found lacking in the moment. And so Bonhoeffer concludes, ethics too is "a matter of history and history is always changing."[6]

However, Bonhoeffer does not wholly reject the notion of principled living, as if its rejection sentences one to individualistic

2. Bethge, *Dietrich Bonhoeffer*, 696.
3. Rasmussen, *Dietrich Bonhoeffer*, 27.
4. Plant, *Bonhoeffer*, 78.
5. *NRS*, 39.
6. Ibid., 40.

expression. The concern for community was too much a theme in his theology. Bethge explains this tension: "[Bonhoeffer] wanted to surmount the abstractness of a normative ethic and still accept its interest in continuity."[7] Bonhoeffer confirms this tension in a letter to friend Hermann Thumm in June 1929: "Principles are quite good, but only until one is taught something better by the language of reality."[8]

The "better," however, does not negate the attempt at principled living but contextualizes it into a proper union with reality, where the language of reality (*Sprache der Tatsachen*) is wholly seated in the concrete world.

Existentialist Ethics

John Frame has called existential ethics "a matter of human inwardness, a matter of character and motive. Ethical behavior, on this view, must not be motivated by external reward, which would be mercenary, or by mere law, which would be drudgery."[9] The question of whether Dietrich Bonhoeffer was an existentialist thinker depends largely upon the degree to which he departs from those thinkers for whom an existential approach was significant.

"The main source for the philosophies of existence is Kierkegaard and especially his category of the subject."[10] And though Bonhoeffer is influenced by existentialist thinkers like Kierkegaard and Nietzsche, especially on the grounds of motivation and character, his ethical method differs on a very important level: the community, not the individual, forms the primary referent of existence. In this way, inwardness is not the goal but togetherness. His famous dictum *Christus als Gemeinde existierend* suggests that intrapersonal relationships take precedent over the individual, the result of which demands that being-for-others can never be abstracted from

---

7. Bethge, *Dietrich Bonhoeffer*, 717.
8. DBWE 10, 1/85, 186.
9. Frame, *Perspectives on the Word of God*, 41.
10. Sanchez and Sanchez, "Jean Wahl," 407.

one's own moral duties. For this reason, Bonhoeffer would find Kierkegaard's knight of faith and Nietzsche's *Übermensch* questionable as final expressions of ethical truth because both of these concepts are wholly invested in the individual (being-for-itself).

As noted in the previous chapter, the Lutheran emphasis on the individual as the subject of God's saving grace becomes for Bonhoeffer the emphasis on Person as the human condition taken up in Jesus. The import of this doctrine extends to ethics insofar as it is based in God's love (as the highest ethic) for humanity. Love compels us to *do* ethics for others. The question of "how can I love God whom I have not seen, and hate my brother whom I have" is more forcefully answered by Bonhoeffer with regard to the concretion of Jesus. In Christ we *have* seen God, and therefore we must love one another. This love is not simply a response to one's brother but is the taking up of his entire being, which has the effect of preventing the concept of Person from being interpreted in isolation before God (Kierkegaard), or as an entirely new view of humanity evolving from the rejection of one's prior self (Nietzsche).

Situation Ethics

The way of doing ethics associated with contextual ethical dilemmas is situation ethics. This approach comes from the work of Joseph Fletcher.[11] Though this approach is historically anachronistic, Fletcher attempts to discover Bonhoeffer in his own approach, citing the latter as someone who anticipates his own work.

According to Fletcher, love occupies the highest rung of one's ethical requirement. There are, however, two important ways in which Bonhoeffer distinguishes his ethic from pure situational priority. Although Bonhoeffer's ethics are contextual, ethical solutions do not arise from the situation in which they are worked out. Rasmussen puts it this way: "The Christian's decisions are also made in a particular *historical* context, the knowledge of which is indispensable for discerning Christ's peculiar *Gestalt* in this time

---

11. Fletcher, *Situation Ethics: The New Morality*, 26.

and place, for uncovering the concrete command of God that will bring reality to expression here and now."[12] The qualification is that while ethical decision making is approached from within the context, it is not dependent upon the context. Rather, ethical decision making, although situated in context, transcends context because it always poses the "question of Christ."

Secondly, Bonhoeffer's ethics must not be confused with the kind of situation ethics brought forth by Fletcher. As Robin Gill notes, "Bonhoeffer sees a sharp divide between ethics and Christian ethics whereas, for Fletcher, Christian and non-Christian situation ethics differ only in the *summum bonum* (highest good) regarded as their standard . . . and, in practice, he moves almost imperceptibly from one discipline to the other."[13] For Bonhoeffer, Christ is not simply the authorization for ethical reflection. Rather, Christ is irrevocably the *method* and *reality* of ethical reflection, that is, there is a place where formal and material distinctions converge. An ethics built on rudimentary life-affirming doctrines can surely be achieved in any number of systems, whether it is peace, charity, or forgiveness; and yet these are imperceptibly distinct from expressions birthed in one's relationship with Christ. Bonhoeffer even rejects any such notion that a Christian principle of love outside of the love that is directly encountered in Christ is authentically Christian. The love of Christ cannot be reduced to a doctrine of love. In a lengthy passage, Bonhoeffer addresses the problem of grounding one's ethical duties in the commandment of love as a uniquely Christian operation:

> We are familiar with the passage in which Jesus is asked about the highest commandment and offers the twofold response, "You shall love the Lord your God with all your heart, and with all your soul, and with all your mind." . . . And a second is like it: "You should love your neighbor as yourself." We also recall Jesus's words concerning love of one's enemies: "Love your enemies, bless those who curse you, do good to those who hate you and pray for

---

12. Rasmussen, *Dietrich Bonhoeffer: Reality and Resistance*, 25.
13. Gill, *Textbook of Christian Ethics*, 38.

those who persecute you, so that you may be children of your Father in heaven; for he makes his sun rise on the evil and on the good, and sends rain on the righteous and on the unrighteous. For if you love those who love you, what reward do you have? Do not even tax collectors do the same?" If the proclamation of this particular commandment really had been the focal point of Jesus's whole ministry, he would have commenced at precisely this point ever anew. But he did not. This same conclusion emerges with unequivocal clarity from a comparison of the words of Jesus with those of Jewish rabbis and pagan philosophers, which often resemble one another even in their wording. When asked what the highest commandment is, Rabbi Hillel responded: "Love your neighbor as yourself. That is the highest commandment." Another advised: "What you would not want to happen to yourself, do not to others." The Roman philosopher Seneca urged us "not to tire of working for the common good, of helping individuals, and of providing help even to our enemies."[14]

In both deontological and situation ethics then, the question of authority remains unresolved. Simply stated, a deontological ethic assumes the question of authority in a general way, which in itself bears nothing distinctively Christian. Likewise, situation ethics ignores the question of authority because what is most important is the result. Existential ethics, with its attention to subjectivity and the individual, ultimately is too narrow to take seriously Bonhoeffer's unique positioning of the community as the context for individual.

Utilitarianism

The attraction of Utilitarianism is its emphasis on the collective. In relation to Bonhoeffer, for whom community is the measure of all ethical application, there would seem to exist a potential for comparison. Aside from this superficiality, the similarity ends. Jeremy

---

14. *DBWE* 10, 2/3, 364.

Bentham, the driving force behind utilitarianism's popular rise in the Anglo-Saxon world, notes that while decisions in this approach are arrived at within the community, the value of utilitarianism derives from its interpretation of the individual. "The community is a fictitious body, composed of the individual persons who are considered as constituting as it were its members. The interest of the community then is, what?—the sum of the interests of several members who compose it."[15]

For Bonhoeffer, the notion of utility is not a modern phenomenon, but an element of Epicureanism. In his estimation, utilitarianism is a deficient view because of its inability to understand the individual at a level other than as an arrangement of interpersonal commerce. "One person is fundamentally alien to the other."[16] Green notes, "A utilitarian approach cannot yield Gemeinschaft, 'community,' as an end in itself, since social forms exist in that view only to serve the happiness of the individual."[17]

A second element working against utilitarianism was its foreign nature. Rejection of utilitarian philosophy is therefore tied to the political reality of Bonhoeffer's Germany. John Anthony Moses notes that German romantic thinkers rejected the mechanistic utilitarian notion of the state and preferred in its place an "organic" notion that treated the individual holistically.[18]

---

15. Bentham, *Utilitarianism*, 6–7.
16. *DBWE* 1, 39.
17. Ibid., 38–39, n. 12.
18. Moses, *Reluctant Revolutionary*, 24; Bonhoeffer makes a similar distinction: "The Anglo-Saxon world today conceives of its struggle against the omnipotence of the state in terms of the concept of freedom. It understands by this the protection of God-given human rights in the face of every violation. Germans perceive the omnipotence of the state more as the arbitrary dissolution of all authentic bonds (family, friendship, home, people, government, humanity, scholarship, work, etc.) and they fight against the omnipotence of the state for the establishment of authentic bonds (*DBWE* 16, 2/11, 531).

BONHOEFFER'S ETHICAL METHOD

Relational-Christological Ethics

Within the structure of Bonhoeffer's method, two approaches manifest. Larry Rasmussen identifies these as follows: *Ethik als Gebot* (command) and *Ethik als Gestalt* (formation), the latter of which is predominant in Bonhoeffer's *Ethics*.[19] While he acknowledges other ways in which Bonhoeffer attempts ethical analysis, Rasmussen writes, it is through these that "Bonhoeffer is most explicit" because "they carry the longest history in his writings."[20]

It is important to attempt a distinction between these two approaches. I believe that this distinction represents emphases that are not substantively different, a point I will discuss below. *Ethik als Gebot* is identified with Bonhoeffer's earliest foray into theological ethics. The main line of emphasis is the command of God. The command should not be confused with commandment theology or Mosaic law. *Ethik als Gebot* does not expose the individual to the right form of action (what Bonhoeffer considers the idealism of commandment ethics) but rather it is ever-before the individual and demands a response as affirmation of the one who gives it.

According to Rasmussen, "the command is a specific, prophetic word to the concrete situation, or it is not God's command; its center is in Christ; and the command itself, if it is truly God's command, corresponds with reality."[21] Thus, the commandment of God must be that which speaks to each individual in his or her present situation.

Conversely, *Ethik als Gestalt* is best expressed as Christ formed in the structure of reality. In Bonhoeffer's earlier ethical writing, in which *Gebot* is the primary mode, the Christological ethic forming the basis of reality is not entirely worked out. Rasmussen writes, "This move from the unique [*Gebot*] to the universal [*Gestalt*], the particular to the general, represents Bonhoeffer's growing insight

---

19. I refer to these as approaches of method. Rasmussen himself refers to these interchangeably as "themes," "approaches," and "treatments." With concern for avoiding semantic looseness, I choose the former (see Rasmussen's use in "Question of Method").

20. Rasmussen, "Question of Method," 103.

21. Ibid., 118.

into the structured ontological unity of the form of the world and the form of Christ. Reality is seen to be Christocractic, shaped by the form of Christ."[22] The *Gestalt* form is often identified with Bonhoeffer's later ethics and in particular with the mandates, which are the pre-ethical obligations imposed upon humanity in various social institutions and orders. As Jürgen Moltmann explains Bonhoeffer's view: "The whole world is created through Christ and unto Christ whether it knows it or not. The world's relation to Christ takes concrete form in a number of divine mandates in which certain basic relationships and spheres of life are shaped and defined."[23]

The question of how *Gebot* and *Gestalt* maintain their relationship model in Bonhoeffer's later work is an important one. Although Hanfried Müller asserts that Bonhoeffer treats these as separate methods,[24] Rasmussen details twelve points of similarity in the approaches and argues that given this shared space it is difficult to see how they qualify as separate methods.[25]

But if not separate, what is intended by this move that deprives their manifestations of any distinction? Likewise, could similarities shared by both approaches permit simultaneous access to ethical problems that continues into Bonhoeffer's *Ethics*? Rasmussen's primary distinction lies in his assertion that Bonhoeffer's ethics "continues to carry its contextualism, but it loses the atomism in increasing measure," so that "although the emphasis on the uniqueness of each ethical context, and therefore each ethical decision, is not denied in the years following, the terms depicting the *sui generis* character of such decisions are replaced by categories of a more general nature."[26] While the new terms of Bonhoeffer's *Gestalt* ethics are introduced, the question of whether this is a replacement requires explanation, which I will address in a later section in this chapter, "Bonhoeffer's Work on *Ethics*."

22. Rasmussen, *Dietrich Bonhoeffer: Reality and Resistance*, 26.
23. Moltmann, "Lordship of Christ and Human Society," 71.
24. Müller, *Von der Kirche zur Welt*, 288–89.
25. Rasmussen, "Question of Method," 135–38.
26. Rasmussen, *Dietrich Bonhoeffer: Reality and Resistance*, 26.

Rasmussen further elaborates that the ethical transformation in Bonhoeffer's thinking is not only the distance between *sui generis* and general approaches but *sui generis* and neo-casuistic thinking. This, too, requires some elaboration.

Rasmussen's comments on the casuistic character of Bonhoeffer's ethical decision making appears to be based on a particular interpretation that considers it a type of formalism due to its association with principle-based thinking. At the same time, Rasmussen notes formalism is something that Bonhoeffer "relentlessly avoids."[27] Bonhoeffer, too, appears to reject casuistry, and states "the concrete Christian ethics stands beyond formalism and casuistry."[28]

Here, I am not so sure one should take Bonhoeffer's objection as a general indictment of casuistry. As Rasmussen seems to confirm, the rejection appears directed at the role *principles* assume as the exhaustive meaning and outcome of casuistic thinking. Part of this is confirmed in Bonhoeffer's notion that the casuistic process always *ends* in failure, because it tries to establish "what is good once and for all"—precisely at which point a principle is reestablished or repristinated. That Bonhoeffer's understanding of casuistry comes from within a particular model, Nigel Biggar suggests, is a rejection of the ethical rationalism that he shares with most Protestants since the seventeenth century. Not only is casuistry not confined to a kind of closed logical system, "casuistry constantly involves the modification of old rules and the generation of new ones in the attempt to give faithful expression to a given moral

---

27. Rasmussen, *Dietrich Bonhoeffer: Reality and Resistance*, 156; Green, who mentions a deleted passage asserting "every ethic between formalism and casuistry," considers casuistry and formalism to be at opposite ends of the ethic spectrum (see also *DBWE* 6, 99–100, n. 106).

28. Ibid., 99, n. 106. Green notes that Bonhoeffer's rejection of this dynamic comes from his experience with the sacrament of the Lutheran confession, where for each confession a formulaic resolution was received. Benjamin T. G. Mayes reaches an opposite conclusion, claiming Bonhoeffer sought to rediscover the divine office of Confession at the time of the Reformation, which Mayes argues was precisely casuistic and absolute (see *Counsel and Conscience*, 41).

principle in reaction to new, morally significant data."[29] In giving expression to the conceptual framework of ethical language that exists in Christianity, Bonhoeffer often reworks concepts like love or peace and locates them within Christ where they are secured from stagnation. Throughout his writings, in case-based scenarios, including exegetical examples, Bonhoeffer represents at the head of his analyses principles as standard interpretations and reworks them into his relational ethic. Indeed, as already noted, Bonhoeffer admits that principles are useful, and later in the *Ethics* gives positive expression to a phrase he locates in Luther in which "rendering obedience, human beings observe God's Decalogue, in exercising freedom, they create new decalogues."[30] The end result need not be a principle, if by this we understand Bonhoeffer's own standard rejection of abstract rules that dominate over humanity. Richard Brian Miller's explanation of modern casuistic thinking is helpful in locating Bonhoeffer's own position, even where Bonhoeffer himself does not.[31] According to Miller, casuistry is a five-stage process in which the rejection of presumptions and the move to new paradigms is designed in order to treat unique subject matter. Similarly, the test and trial of presumptuous ethical thinking is often a theological starting point in Bonhoeffer's own engagement with concrete reality. Bonhoeffer's method for moving through unique (*sui generis*) ethical dilemmas leads to the paradigm of Christ's person, which has the effect of being interpretatively inexhaustible. What becomes paradigmatic in Bonhoeffer's Christological method then is not that Christ sets up or even becomes a new rule to invalidate old ones, but that his very presence is the justification for a dynamic relationship wherein one does his ethical thinking that was otherwise previously closed off.

It is interesting to note that Fletcher recognized what he considered to be confusion in Bonhoeffer's understanding of casuistry.[32] What Rasmussen appears to have in mind with regard to

29. Biggar, *Hastening that Waits*, 41.
30. *DBWE* 6, 288.
31. Miller, *Casuistry and Modern Ethics*, 5.
32. Fletcher, *Situation Ethics*, 149.

the neo-casuistic character of Bonhoeffer's later writing then is the reintroduction of principles in formation (*Gestaltung*). Rasmussen refers to Heinrich Ott, who in writing about *Ethik als Gestalt*, states that this is the "*oberstes materielles Prinzip dieser Ethik.*"[33] Nevertheless, in an important section entitled "Ethics as Formation," Bonhoeffer states that both Christ and God must also not be treated as principles.[34] Because Bonhoeffer also depicts Christ *as* reality, the logic of identification is not wholly satisfying.[35] Thus, Bonhoeffer's rejection of casuistry is a rejection of a certain conclusion reached in casuistic thinking prominent in his day, even while he unknowingly shares the types of concrete situations and some of the logical process through which casuistic thinking is directed.

It is not clear how the concept of *atomism* is applied by Rasmussen, except that he seems to use it interchangeably with the *sui generis* character of ethical decision making. Since he does not define it directly, I will assume Rasmussen means a sort of insularity limited by individual interpretation that lends itself to the absolute uniqueness of the individual's ethical horizon.

Because *Ethik als Gestalt* does not evolve independent of *Ethik als Gebot*, and given the preceding analysis, it is my assertion that greater emphasis in favor of *Ethik als Gestalt* in his latter writing does not affect the way Bonhoeffer considers the issues of peace and violence.

---

33. Ott, *Wirklichkeit und Glaube*, 241. It should be noted that in Bonhoeffer's discussion on reality in *Ethics*, he admits a false reality that exists alongside the reality of Christ. This echoes similar thoughts found in an earlier work in which he speaks of the difference between inauthentic principles of moral virtue and those found in God.

34. *DBWE* 6, 98–99.

35. "*Es gibt daher nicht zwei Räume, sondern nur den einen Raum der Christuswirklichkeit, in dem Gottes- und Weltwirklichkeit miteinander vereinigt sind*" (*DBW* 6:43).

Early Dimensions of Bonhoeffer's Ethical Method

The argument that Bonhoeffer did not develop a formal sensitivity to Christian ethics prior to the early 1930s seems to ignore the important lessons he learned as a young man between two wars. Bonhoeffer's ethics has the advantage of looking in two directions: both to the then-recent past, in which he tries to make sense of a post-war Germany, and to the future as it will come to pass in the form of National Socialism. Elements that are integral to his ethical method in his latter days can be recognized in some of his earliest attempts at critical analysis.

Prior to the structural bond he creates with his more expanded view of Christology, Bonhoeffer is clearly attracted to relationship as being the starting point of all ethics. Where the concept is particularly at home is in Bonhoeffer's affection for sensate, that is, intentional living in the immediate world. Two early essays, written while he was still a student, give a taste of this affection. In the first, he compares the Latin poet Catullus to his contemporary Horace: "Horace is, in essence, a poet who wrote descriptive, interpretive, and finally contemplative lyrics. Catullus is the exact opposite. In the blink of an eye he throws verses on paper; soon afterward they could be forgotten. One can't imagine him as a philosopher."[36]

Catullus is markedly more interested in the world that lies about him than is Horace, the champion of heady verse. Bonhoeffer's final assessment that the worldly Catullus was the more authentic of the two was met with reproof by his instructor, Walther Kranz, who extolled the virtues of idealism: "Emotion is 'noise and smoke.' Art remains forever . . . And it is an eternal *truth!*"[37]

In the winter semester of 1924–1925, Bonhoeffer wrote a critical analysis on the Jewish influence found in the post-apostolic letter of First Clement. Here, Bonhoeffer finds another champion of the anti-speculative sort who is "purely practical," for whom "theoretical interests . . . play only a historical role for him . . ."[38] What is

---

36. *DBWE* 9, 2/2, 203.
37. Ibid., 2/2, 214, n. 155.
38. Ibid., 2/2, 241.

striking in his analysis of Clement is the way in which Bonhoeffer conceives of the author as a prototypical Protestant who finds his virtue with regard to election in Christ. This analysis prefigures Bonhoeffer's lifelong interest in the insufficiency of moral systems that are undermined in God. Here, Bonhoeffer concludes that not only are works not a means of salvation for Clement but the very effort of identifying good and evil works is equally of no intrinsic value because only God can justify in the final matter. To argue this, Bonhoeffer notes how God calls creation a "good deed," a meaning that is clearly not intended in an ethical sense. In quoting Clement, the tension is more acute: "whether or not God allows us to do good or evil, everything is in God's hand."[39] One cannot help but read an ominous portent in Bonhoeffer's participation in the plot against Hitler, and the advice he gives to pastors serving on the front lines who feared compromising their offices: "Let us look together to the work of God, which does not stand still regardless of how we participate in it, to God's work in us, in the church, in the whole world."[40] Bonhoeffer concludes that for Clement, the dissolution of good and evil is not the result of immorality, nor a kind of nihilism, but rather the inheritance of Christianity.[41]

An early academic attempt at constructive theology can be found in a paper delivered in Seeberg's seminar at this time entitled, "The Historical and Pneumatological Interpretation of Scripture." The paper begins with a point that, when compared to latter work, provides a signpost for the importance of theological context and concretion. Bonhoeffer writes that "Christian religion stands or falls with the belief in a historical and perceptibly real divine revelation."[42] As a historically valid mode of existential awareness, revelation is not an otherworldly imposition on reality but exists in the "free composition" of Christ. He explores this issue by raising the question of a legitimate epistemological method

39. Ibid., 2/4, 244.
40. *DBWE* 16, 1/6, 47.
41. For a discussion on the overcoming of good and evil, see the section on Nietzsche in chapter 1.
42. *DBWE* 9, 2/6, 285.

adopted by the contemporary scientific-mechanistic worldview as one which has a tendency to compartmentalize, while carrying within itself the claim that "knowledge should be attainable for every reasonable person by separating, in principle, the knowing subject and known object."[43] The critical rejection of this statement is one of methodological consideration and anticipates his own theological worldview. So it is also true that Bonhoeffer's attack on an *In Principiis* approach to theology draws not from the individual's knowledge of God, as though what comes with this is a guarantee of moral or epistemic absolutes, but from a particular worldview. In declaring universally valid truths, science nurtures a knowable world as justification for its own relevance. This runs the danger and risks the hubris of becoming a negative metaphysic that extends beyond the realm of empirical knowledge. Further, such a view imposes a boundary condition upon the experience of reality, not only from a historically bound frame of reference but also as a diminution of humanity to a particular kind of analysis.[44]

In his paper, this infiltration is primarily confined to the reading of Scripture. At this early stage, Bonhoeffer understands that the discussion is about methodology. Indeed, these early reflections favor revelation as the filter whereby concrete reality must reject subservience to a scientific interpretation of life.

> We must say a priori that it is unacceptable for a pneumatological, faith-based interpretation to be dependent upon historical methods of reading scripture with their shifting results. The difficulty rises from the fact that belief cannot free itself from the [Word became flesh], nor does it want to. On the other hand, the historian's sense of truth cannot tolerate any patronizing by foreign methods. None of us can return to a pre-critical time. Both methods are used side by side by any pneumatological interpreter.[45]

43. Ibid., 2/6, 286.

44. Bonhoeffer denies a naturalistic theology in favor of *kerygma*. In this same essay, the relationship to Barth's discussion on *Menschenwort* and *Gotteswort* is pointed out.

45. Ibid., 2/6, 294.

Bonhoeffer's Ethical Method

I would argue that the recommendation here is not that a reciprocal relationship between the two methodologies occur, only that the two cannot ignore each other. Bonhoeffer's early attempts then to analyze an approach through the "Word became flesh," while at the same time affirming the conclusions of modern biblical criticism, is a tribute to the kind of academic theology that maintained the core of its own relevance in the world, rather than being at odds with it. What is critical here is that Bonhoeffer represents context and concretion, and more directly "belief," as features in which the Word reveals and takes shape in this world. He identifies this as a method. Later, the word "method" is no longer used. One wonders if this occurred out of a fear of rigidity implied in the word itself or out of concern that such a use trends to the side of the more process-heavy approach of textual criticism whose influence he was attempting to control. Nonetheless, his method continues in the body of his work, whether expressed as such or not.

During his year in Barcelona, Bonhoeffer's attention turned to the commandment of God. *Commandment* for Bonhoeffer is not an abstract principle of behavior. His most important reflections on ethics at this time come in a sermon entitled "Basic Questions of a Christian Ethic" This sermon was the third in a three-part series and was delivered during the close of his apprenticeship in the Barcelona congregation to which he was assigned. Rasmussen identified this sermon as an example of methodological atomism, and I reproduce the passage, which Rasmussen also does in his own work. Said Bonhoeffer:

> From all this it now follows that the content of ethical problems can never be discussed in a Christian light; the possibility of erecting generally valid principles simply does not exist, because each moment, lived in God's sight, can bring an unexpected decision. Thus only one thing can be repeated again and again, also in our time: in ethical decisions a man must consider his action *sub*

specie aeternitatis and then, no matter how it proceeds, it will proceed rightly.[46]

The relational dimension of Bonhoeffer's ethical decision making arises in what he calls the face-to-face encounter with God. In an essay for Reinhold Niebuhr at Union Theological Seminary, he considers the problem of religious determinism in relation to authentic ethical encounters with God.

> Here we are dealing not with an interpretation of the world but with the question concerning human beings and their situation before God . . . Rather than engaging a certain idea of God in interpreting what happens in the world, here we expect an answer to our question from the real God. Rather than already knowing the answer beforehand [here Bonhoeffer is referring to his interpretation of religious determinism that asserts that there is always cause for all things], the human being expects it from outside, from God. This changes the whole picture. God and human being stand facing each other, as person and person. Human beings believe themselves to be placed by God before the question of existence and must hear the answer from God.[47]

Similar language prior to this comes at the end of a lecture he gave in Barcelona on the problem of identifying the origin of an ethical command. Here Bonhoeffer describes what is essential to the ethical decision-making process: "The significance of all of Jesus' commandments is rather to say to people: You stand before the face of God. God's grace rules over you; but you are at the disposal of someone else in the world. You must act and behave such that in each of your actions you are mindful of also acting before God, mindful that God has a certain will and wants to see that will done."[48]

---

46. Rasmussen draws his quote from *NRS*, 45–46 (cf. *DBWE* 10, 2/3, 368).
47. *DBWE* 10, 2/14, 442–43.
48. Ibid., 2/3, 365.

The ideas here of one's proximity (the individual acting before God) and favor (grace ruling over the individual) are part of Bonhoeffer's approach to a relational ethic. Duty is not of primary consideration because the commandments are not meant to point us to universal ethical standards but reflect our relational being in the world. This is a constant theme in Bonhoeffer's work. One such example comes from a series of lectures that Bonhoeffer delivered at the University of Berlin between 1932 and 1933, which became the impetus for his work *Creation and Fall*. Here Bonhoeffer suggests that the story of Genesis represents the ethical relationship between man and God that is ontologically prior to man's knowledge of good and evil. This relationship is only later challenged through the antagonism of the serpent.

The Individual and Other as Ground of Ethical Relationships

Bonhoeffer's Christological ethical method cannot be fully appreciated without a discussion of the concept of Person, especially as it was being discussed in the German academy during Bonhoeffer's tenure. In a July 31, 1930, lecture delivered in Berlin, Bonhoeffer reflects on the question of being human, calling it "one of the most passionately posed questions in contemporary philosophy."[49] He summarizes the views on the anthropological question in the work of Max Scheler, Martin Heidegger, Paul Tillich, and Eberhard Grisebach. The underlying similarity expressed by these thinkers is how the individual understands himself in his or her world (with perhaps Scheler as the exception) and what corresponding actions accompany this understanding. A basic theme explored here by Bonhoeffer through these thinkers is the rejection of the individual as essential being (*Wesen*) contrasted with one who is "understood from his possibilities" in the dynamism of his existence.[50] Bonhoeffer provides his own analysis of these thinkers'

---

49. Ibid., 2/7, 392.
50. Ibid., 2/7, 393.

individual positions and offers his critique. Whether one accepts the correctness of Bonhoeffer's critique is not as important as recognizing how the critique leads Bonhoeffer to posit his own view. Bonhoeffer's problem with Max Scheler is that Scheler creates a material *a priori* world of values transcending human consciousness that cannot accommodate what Bonhoeffer calls the suddenly erupting reality of the demonic world of human desires.[51] Bonhoeffer, who engages Heidegger in *Act and Being*, analyzes the concept of *Dasein* (being-there) as the subject who finds himself in a world. Although Bonhoeffer rejects Heidegger's conclusion that the move from inauthentic to authentic existence comes by way of *Dasein*'s own power, he nonetheless admires Heidegger's relational notion of "*Dasein* as care" (*Sorge*).[52] Furthermore, *Dasein*'s concrete being in the world with others (*Mitsein mit Anderen*) rejects any idealistic portrayal of human existence, and this observation is key to Bonhoeffer's own ethical approach.

Bonhoeffer reads Tillich as one who builds upon Heidegger. In his lecture, Bonhoeffer associates both Tillich and Heidegger with acting in the moment, in which the individual must choose himself. While the human for Heidegger is oriented towards his project of overcoming the boundary conditions of life (e.g., death), Tillich sees any unified theory of the Person as being an impossible task. Bonhoeffer sees Heidegger's individual finding himself by looking inwardly, while Tillich's individual owes any concept of validation to his complete reliance on the eternal, for he "protests against all human self-positing and securing."[53]

---

51. Ibid.; Bonhoeffer might be eluding to the developing field of psychoanalysis in the person of Sigmund Freud, whose theories challenged the psychological legitimacy of the religious life.

52. Ibid., 2/7, 396–97; Bonhoeffer also rejects Heidegger because he feels Heidegger's philosophy leads to an isolation that cuts *Dasein* off from others and the world itself. "The question becomes the answer; the human being basically knows about himself; the question has no ultimate seriousness." In the concept of *Sorge für Anderen*, Bonhoeffer admires Heidegger but is not confident that Heidegger's case is compelling given the limitation of isolation mentioned above.

53. Ibid., 2/7, 398.

Bonhoeffer's Ethical Method

Bonhoeffer contends that it is Grisebach, however, who moves from the individual to other persons, and so is closest to his own considerations. Bonhoeffer's emphasis on community in *Sanctorum Communio* takes up with Grisebach the necessity of others for determining oneself. As Bonhoeffer writes, "What is really new in Grisebach's position is that he cannot conceive the human being apart from the concrete other person."[54] Finally, Bonhoeffer's brief mention of Friedrich Gogarten is offered to correct the impulse to absolutize one's neighbor in place of God. For Bonhoeffer, this misstep removes the importance of revelation and replaces it with an "inner-worldly ethic," for which the only ground that can be supposed is the human.[55]

In Bonhoeffer's estimation, however, all these views suffer in so far as they set up a boundary as the condition of authentic living. By contrast, Bonhoeffer thinks such boundaries must presuppose that the individual has already violated the boundary in order to know it.[56] The result is that human beings cannot act as self-determining beings. Neither can they direct their reality toward a sufficient explanation of what it means to be human. The one asking the question needs something other than himself for validation, even beyond the existence of another person. What does a legitimate encounter with this *other* look like? Recalling his criticism of Heidegger, Bonhoeffer describes the situation as follows: "The human being is torn completely out of himself, drawn as a whole person before God, and here the question about the human being becomes serious precisely because it no longer includes its own answer."[57] If this is true, understanding what it means to be human through one's own possibilities (a tenet of existentialism) is also inappropriate because these possibilities originate inwardly.

The answer for Bonhoeffer is revelation. To speak of one's capacity to receive revelation undermines its effect because it would

---

54. Ibid.
55. Ibid., 2/7, 402.
56. Ibid., 2/7, 399.
57. Ibid., 2/7, 400.

not be entirely something outside the individual (via Barth).⁵⁸ Only revelation that comes from God tears the individual from self-reflection and conceives of him something entirely new. Bonhoeffer recognizes this as the fundamental difference between philosophy and theological anthropology. Although Bonhoeffer's Christology has not yet occupied the central motif of his ethics, his thinking is clear: the encounter beyond oneself is through Christ.⁵⁹

With this, Bonhoeffer reaffirms from *Sanctorum Communio* the preeminence of community over individual. The fact that he moves in his lecture through a series of philosophical and theological solutions is evidence that Bonhoeffer saw qualitative similarities in the search for the Person he aligned with Barth to reject philosophical inquiry as the primary method for interpreting the Person (*contra* Bultmann).⁶⁰

The Direction of Ethics: Christ for Others

The concepts of "being-for-the-person" and "Christ for others" were broached in the previous chapter because of Bonhoeffer's attempt to join himself to the theological tradition he sees represented in Luther. Christ as *pro me / pro nobis* denotes the relational dimension of Bonhoeffer's ethics in which Christ becomes humanity (*Menschwerdung*) as an ethical rather than an epistemological concept. The peculiarity of the human body Christ occupies is of limited importance to Bonhoeffer. In Bonhoeffer's view, the human body of Christ merely makes way for the individual sense of person to be taken up in the corporate person. By contrast, for Bonhoeffer, the ethical application of the "for-otherness" of Christ, which takes up the individual as well, means that ethics are never exercised without regard for the community. In a late entry, Bonhoeffer explains the category of *Dasein-für-andere*, which shows

58. Ibid., 2/7, 403.

59. Ibid.; "The human being perceives the claim of the neighbor as the absolute only if God's absolute claim in Christ has encountered him and given him the answer to the question about himself."

60. Webster, *Cambridge Companion to Karl Barth*, 27.

the continued importance of the concept for his ethical methodology. *"Unser Verhältnis zu Gott ist kein religiöses zu einem denkbar höchsten, mächtigsten, besten Wesen—dies ist kein echte Transzendenz—, sondern unser Verhältnis zu Gott ist ein neues Leben im Dasein-für-andere, in der Teilnahme am Sein Jesus."*[61] Dasein's "being there" for Bonhoeffer, as with Heidegger, has the implication of a being engaged in its activity and not simply as a mere fact of life. Dasein is concrete, but it is also aware.[62]

Movement Toward Christological Ethics

While Bonhoeffer's Christological ethics is not formally worked out in the early 1930s, the move toward a more robust appreciation of an ethics that places Christ at the center of human activity is expressed through his work in the ecumenical movement. In July 1932, at the Youth Peace Conference in Czechoslovakia, Bonhoeffer makes an important attempt to identify Christ as the inextricable ground and justification of the church. Here Bonhoeffer frames the reality of Christ as the very structure of the church.

> The church is the presence of Christ on earth, the church is the *Christus praesens*. For this reason alone its word has authority. The word of the church is the word of the present Christ, it is gospel and commandment. It would be the retrogression of the church to the synagogue if its proclamation were commandment alone, and it would be the lapse of the church into libertinism should it want to deny the commandment of God for the sake of the Gospel.[63]

61. "Our relationship with God is no religious relationship to a highest, most powerful, best being imaginable—this is no real transcendence—rather our relationship to God is a new life in being-there for the Other, in the participation of Christ's being" (my translation). (*DBW* 8:558).

62. Rasmussen notes that *Fuer-andere-Dasein* is always qualified as *Fuer-andere-Dasein Jesu* in Bonhoeffer's theology. *Dietrich Bonhoeffer: Reality and Resistance*, 170.

63. NRS, 161.

Aside from pointing to the importance of establishing the social dimension of the church, there is a second level of theological analysis that can be noted.[64] By his phrase "commandment alone," one must keep in mind Bonhoeffer's continued rejection of abstract commandments, which are always outside of Christ. Bonhoeffer insists that the Christ presented through the concrete gospel frees us from the indetermination of such commandments. At the same time, Bonhoeffer wants to reject a scenario in which one claims the Christ of the gospel but denies obedience to his commandment, as if one could treat Christ's life as something that happened outside of time and so remain unaffected. In this way too, Bonhoeffer critiques the church for its obstinacy to move into the public square and act on hard ethical issues. The commandment and gospel are incomplete in themselves unless they are grounded in the very presence of Christ. That Christ is both interpreted in commandment and gospel means that, as God's word, Christ occupies the same space. In doing so Christ domesticates transcendence, so that the two cannot exist apart. Bonhoeffer builds upon his early work in *Sanctorum Communio* to note that when these concepts are moderated by obedience, then any ethical dilemma, approached in faith, is not only answered in our being before God but takes on further meaning in that the present Christ is alive in his relationship to us.

Bonhoeffer insists that *Christus praesens* must not be understood as a model by which the church operates, but as the very orientation of the community. "Christ is not in-himself and also in the church-community, but the Christ who is the only Christ is the one present in the church-community *pro-me*."[65] In this way, Bonhoeffer de-prioritizes the speculative question of "What

---

64. Bonhoeffer's point here is clearly a critique directed against the then-current theological foundation that formed in defense of the National Socialist state. This critique answers statements such as the Ansbach Reply, which Pierard notes, "distinguishes between gospel (the message of Jesus Christ who died for our sins and was raised for our justification) and law (the immutable will of God that meets us in the totality of life)" ("The Lutheran Two-Kingdoms Doctrine," 201).

65. *DBWE* 12, 2/12, 314.

is the nature of Christ?" and instead expresses "Who is Christ in the church?" With the writing of his *Ethics*, Bonhoeffer broadens the concept of community to include the world. Nevertheless, the fundamentals remain the same: "*Christus ist für die Welt gestorben, und nur mitten in der Welt ist Christus Christus.*"[66]

Reflecting this concept of *Christus praesens*, in 1933, Bonhoeffer writes of Christ as follows: "The one who is present in Word, sacrament and community is in the center of human existence, history and nature. It is part of his structure that he stands in the center."[67]

In his lectures in Berlin that are based upon transcribed notes from his student Gerhard Riemer, Bonhoeffer is said to have distinguished humanity's proper ethical orientation as being between who Christ *is* and what Christ *does*.[68] Rejecting the interpretation that Christ is a power that can be accessed at will, or that one apprehends his person through his works, Riemer's transcription states, "only where the risen Christ is understood as the ground and the prerequisite for Christology is it possible to grasp his presence as person."[69] "Presence" is not a metaphysical claim here, but a relational one. The nature of this *pro me* relationship of Christ "is not to be understood as an effect that issues from Christ or as a form that he assumes incidentally, but is to be understood as the being of his very person. This is not a historical, factual, or ontic statement but rather an ontological one: that is, I can never think of Jesus Christ in his being-in-himself, but only in his relatedness to me."[70] So, too, this ethical formation of Christ for a person, including his demands upon a person's life, takes its shape in that person's being toward others. As Green notes, "The person is a socio-ethical,

---

66. "Christ has died for the world, and only within the world is Christ, Christ" (my translation). (*DBW* 6:52).
67. Bonhoeffer, *Christ the Center*, 62.
68. *DBWE* 12, 2/12, 299.
69. Ibid., 2/12, 312.
70. Ibid., 2/12, 314.

historical being whose identity is formed in such ethical encounters with others."[71] The person remains an ethical reality.

Bonhoeffer's Work on *Ethics*

The full maturation of Bonhoeffer's Christological ethics is worked out in his intended, though unfinished, *magnum opus*. In *Ethics*, Bonhoeffer emphasizes the concept of responsibility where obedience once stood. Mediating between these is the concept of freedom.[72]

Throughout this work, Bonhoeffer's theology presents a much deeper engagement of the person of Christ. Green notes it is Bonhoeffer's intention to present the God-man as *Menschwerdung* rather than *Inkarnation*, and Green calls this the methodological starting point in *Ethics*.[73] This decision recalls objections raised

71. Green, "Human sociality and Christian community," 115.

72. Rasmussen has characterized the relationship in *Discipleship* between responsibility and obedience; and in *Ethics* between freedom and responsibility, claiming that this opens the exception for Tyrannicide. (*Dietrich Bonhoeffer: Reality and Resistance*, 50). My own opinion is that because responsibility (*Verantwortung*) represents the secularization of Bonhoeffer's expanding awareness in his theology of the ethical dominion of Christ, responsibility is not developed as a theological component of his methodology until the *Ethics*, while freedom remains a serviceable concept both in one's freedom to obey (*Discipleship*) and in one's freedom for responsibility (*Ethics*). I will discuss this more completely in chapter 4.

73. As far back as the 1933 lectures, Bonhoeffer prefers *Menschgewordene* (became human) to *Menschwerdung* (becoming human) for describing Christ. He does so to avoid speculations about the nature of the incarnation, being that Bonhoeffer sees the latter term dangerously close to an association with the epistemological concern of "how" Christ becomes human, though the latter term is not completely off limits in its usage (see *DBWE* 12, 2/12, 355). The former term indicates that Christ not only took on human flesh, but took humanity into himself. Commenting on the use of the word in the *Ethics*, Green sees the importance of *Menschwerdung* as one that emphasizes "humanity and humanization." "God's becoming human in Jesus Christ not only discloses something about God, namely, God's being-for-humanity; God's being-for-humanity has a purpose and an end." (*DBWE* 6, 6). Both words enjoy emphasis in earlier and later work. Although Rasmussen suggests *Menschwerdung* poses the wrong Christological question during the Berlin years, when expressed

from the Christology lectures in Berlin, in which Bonhoeffer sought to strip the doctrine of its more metaphysically driven goal of uncovering the way in which Christ becomes human, and in so doing focus on Christ's "humanity and humanization."[74] In this way, one understands the doctrine of the incarnation with greater sensitivity to the phrase "the Word made flesh" as opposed to solitary emphasis on a high Christology of the Word, in which the duty of Christ bearing flesh becomes secondary.

But the most important progression in Bonhoeffer's thinking is the formulation of the ethical Christ who is not only the ground that sustains the church, but the ethical reality of the world as well. In the opening pages of *Ethics*, Bonhoeffer expresses this direction: "*Das Problem der christlichen Ethik ist das Wirklichwerden der Offenbarungwirklichkeit Gottes in Christus unter seinen Geschöpfen, wie das Problem der Dogmatik die Wahrheit der Offenbarungswirklichkeit Gottes in Christus ist.*"[75]

No longer is Christ solely the inheritance of the church. Now he stands as the ethical reality of creation itself. It might be reasonably ventured that Bonhoeffer's emphasis on Christ as the *Offenbarungswirklichkeit* was motivated by more than a purely intellectual interest to rework and expand the range of Christ's ethical activity. Bonhoeffer's discontent with the Confessing Church had grown, and by 1936 the church had, in Bonhoeffer's view, acquiesced to the Reich. Bonhoeffer's activities were now largely confined to the secular realm while he worked alongside nominal religious and non-religious companions in the planning and execution of conspiratorial activities.[76] The benefit of expanding Christ's role into the secular realm surely allowed Bonhoeffer some peace of mind in forming an intellectual basis for his activities.

---

positively, *Menschwerdung* shows up in the earlier work of Bonhoeffer in the context of revelation (*DBWE* 12, 45-46).

74. *DBWE* 6, 6.

75. "The problem of Christian ethics is the way in which the reality of the revelation of God is becoming real in Christ amongst his creation, just as the problem of dogmatics is the truth of the reality of the revelation of God in Christ" (my translation). (*DBW* 6:34).

76. Bethge, *Dietrich Bonhoeffer: A Biography*, 718.

Some of the issues raised by *Ethics* are directly associated with the *Sitz im Leben* in Germany. Although Bonhoeffer never attempts to formulate an absolute distinction between the two kingdoms of Christ's activity, and thereby maintaining that distinction's undivided reality, Bonhoeffer's Christology, motivated by the sociological critique he first applied to the church, becomes methodologically proper in both secular and sacred affairs.[77] At the same time, Bonhoeffer countered the Nazi doctrine of *Lebensraum*, one of the motivational ideologies of Hitler's move to annex lands from neighboring countries.[78] The concept of an undivided Christ was not new for Bonhoeffer—he had worked out this concept in other areas of his theology, particularly with regard to the world reconciled through Christ.[79] Because reconciliation of the world is something that Bonhoeffer considered to be an act that had already been completed in Christ, the concept of an undivided Christ here suggests that Bonhoeffer was not breaking with the contextualism and commandment-based ethic that he had heretofore reserved for the church. Rather, this concept, emerging with a more robust formulation, ensured that Christ was extended to the world also.

So, too, Bonhoeffer rejected any consideration that this double reality would only appear as a mental phenomenon that one must be persuaded to adopt. "The character of the statement about [Christ's] centrality is not psychological, but ontological-theological."[80] It matters little whether one believes or accepts it. Again, the concept is not entirely fresh for Bonhoeffer, and can be traced back to his 1933 lectures.[81]

77. Nevertheless, *Ethics* breaks with the rather obsequious tone of "The Church and the Jewish Question" (*DBWE* 12, 2/13) wherein he sees that the Church has limited access to the rule of government (cf. 2/11 "Thy Kingdom Come! The Prayer of the Church-Community for God's Kingdom on Earth").

78. Weinberg, *Hitler's Foreign Policy 1933–1939*, 23–24.

79. *DBWE* 6, 74 and 82 (cf. *DBWE* 4, 257)

80. Robertson [introduction]: Bonhoeffer, *Christ the Center*, 62.

81. As Bonhoeffer writes, "*Mitte unserer Existenz ist nicht Mitte unserer Persönlichkeit. Die Aussage ist nicht psychologisch sondern ontologisch-theologischer Art, in dem sie sich nicht auf unsere Persönlichkeit, sondern auf unsere*

Bonhoeffer's Ethical Method

While Bonhoeffer admits that there are those who wish to maintain a "false reality" in which Christ is not central to reality, he notes that the Christian interpretation of reality is not akin to a "religious perfecting of the profane world."[82] In this way, the question of competing worldviews does not invite an apologetic defense because Christ's reality is already decided. Either way, the ultimate soteriological implications of such a view are uninteresting, and Bonhoeffer's *Ethics* is hardly taken up with the concern.

Along these lines that connect the boundaries between secular and sacred realms of activity is Bonhoeffer's interpretatively difficult concept of a religionless Christianity. Rasmussen suggests the possibility that since the world is in Christ, Bonhoeffer's ethics now have potential application to non-Christians. Here, Rasmussen writes, "because the coherence of God's reality and the world's reality in Christ is ontological, the form of Christ in the world, the real, is ultimately open to apprehension and acknowledgement by every man."[83] Although there are strong elements here leaning toward a kind of Christian universalism, for Bonhoeffer the privilege enjoyed by those who acknowledge the reality of Christ casts doubt on an equivalent experience of religious or spiritual illumination enjoyed by those who do not know Christ by name but who are nevertheless committed to his ethical form in the world.[84] It should be mentioned that Rasmussen only recognizes a broader revelation of the divine as a possible implication in *Ethics*. The problem becomes even more complicated because Rasmussen notes that the move to *Gestalt* in Bonhoeffer's theology is the move from the particular to the general. If by this Rasmussen means to assign the form of Christ recognized in the church to the world as well, then I believe there is evidence. But if this also signals a move to a kind of Christian universalism, it seems that such a claim does not satisfactorily resolve how *Gebot* and *Gestalt* Christology remain

---

Person vor Gott bezieht. Christus ist nicht die vorfindliche Mitte, sondern die geglaubte Mitte" (*DBW* 12:307).

82. *DBWE* 6, 48–49.

83. Rasmussen, *Dietrich Bonhoeffer: Reality and Resistance*, 23.

84. *DBWE* 6, 316.

cohesive, as Rasmussen himself previously suggests, in which the former is eventually worked out in favor of the latter, unless there is something about formation that is decidedly distinct.

As discussed in the previous section, although it is true that Bonhoeffer's view of Christ takes on "theocratic breadth," there is good evidence that Christ continues to occupy real historical space: "*Christentum entspringt aus der Begegnung mit einem konkreten Menschen: Jesus.*"[85] Furthermore, there are examples in *Ethics* where the *Gestalt* Christ synthesizes the historical task. Bonhoeffer writes, "What can and must be said is not what is good once and for all, but the way in which Christ takes form among us here and now."[86] If the form (*Gestalt*) of Christ is not once and for all, then how is his form conceived to be the very ground of existence?

This question of whether Bonhoeffer's contextualism is secondary, as Rasmussen characterizes the issue, depends largely on the way one considers the "new emphasis" (to quote Bethge)[87] as either a matter of course in Bonhoeffer's methodology, which remains finely tuned to the consistency of his own contextualism, or as a diminution of previous ideas with regard to this direction. If such an argument is made with regard to the greater number of features retained in *Ethics* as compared to his earlier work, then the methodological consistency is striking. Bonhoeffer's Christology still is relational insofar as one's face-to-face encounter with God (via Barcelona) is precisely the face of Christ. Thus, Bonhoeffer notes "we experience and recognize ethical reality not by craftiness, not by knowing all the tricks, but only by standing straightforwardly in the truth of God and by looking to that truth with eyes that it makes simple [*einfältig*] and wise." [88]

---

85. "Christianity originates from the encounter with a concrete person: Jesus" (my translation). (Rasmussen, *Dietrich Bonhoeffer: Reality and Resistance*, 28).

86. *DBWE* 6, 85.

87. Bethge, *Dietrich Bonhoeffer: A Biography*, 622.

88. *DBWE* 6, 78. This is most likely a reference to his reading of Matthew 6:22 where it is mentioned in *Discipleship*. The verse from Luther's Bible (1912) reads: "*Das Auge ist des Leibes Licht. Wenn dein Auge einfältig ist, so wird dein ganzer Leib licht sein.*" The German editors note that Απλους in the Greek can

Bonhoeffer's Ethical Method

The ethical categories of good and evil also remain prominent criteria to be rejected. Here, I refer to one example out of many:

> All that has been said thus far implies that we have abandoned the abstract notion, largely dominant in ethical thought, of an isolated individual who has an available absolute criterion by which to choose continually and exclusively between a clearly recognized good and a clearly recognized evil. Such an isolated individual does not exist; nor do we have such an absolute criterion of the good simply at our disposal; nor do good and evil present themselves to us in their pure form.[89]

Obedience in Bonhoeffer's Ethics

The question of obedience for Bonhoeffer is answered in submission to Christ. This question likewise serves as the basis for all subsequent interactions with Christological ethics. How Bonhoeffer's ethical method appropriates the notion of obedience is first formulated negatively as a rejection of ethical principles. In this formulation, human activity is defined within the parameters of good and evil. The idea gains its fullest expression in *Discipleship* (1935–1937). In this work, Bonhoeffer articulates *ethos* by what he calls simple obedience (*einfach Gehorsam*).[90] Bonhoeffer, through his analysis of the serpent's problematic question ("Did God really say?") that seeks to challenge God's authority, had already anticipated the question of obedience in *Creation and Fall*. In this work, the serpent's question is meant to raise doubt with regard to a principle of ethical justice that is itself beyond God. The serpent's words serve to divide Adam with regard to God's real intentions.

---

mean "simple" or "single." It is interesting that the idea of simple obedience is a possible response that transcends the concepts of good and evil in *Ethics* as well as in *Discipleship*. Even as far back as 1932, and prior to *Discipleship*, Bonhoeffer was preparing the ground for simple obedience (e.g., "*Der einfältige Gehorsam weiß nicht von Gut und Böse . . .*" (*DBW* 17:118).

89. *DBWE* 6, 219.
90. *DBWE* 4, 84.

Confusion sweeps in further. As a result, Adam doubts his relationship with God and is led to believe that their unity, which exists in a division defined by obedience (man in the image rather than likeness of God), is somehow less preferable to a relationship that grants him the wisdom to determine the ethical division (*das Zweifache*) between good and evil. In allowing the obedient relationship Adam has with God to be questioned, in hearing the serpent's promise of *sicut deus*, in judging good and evil motives, the consequences for Adam, and indeed humanity, are disastrous. Adam indeed achieves a kind of erroneous moral division, but to his own alienation because it is suggested by Bonhoeffer's argument that the true split (*Zweispalt*) in the individual is not in any way satisfied by grappling the many ways good and evil are defined. At the core, the individual's split is a kind of pre-ethical comprehension of his reality. There is a sense that the individual is not entirely fallen and reasonable evidence to infer Bonhoeffer's channeling of Luther (*finitum capax infinitum*). The pre-ethical division provides the individual his constitution through which concepts like good and evil are surrendered for Nietzschean aesthetics of pleasure and pain.[91] The justice Adam sought in the knowledge of good and evil toward a greater obedience is therefore misguided. Bonhoeffer's analysis here is aimed at the modern dilemma of self-knowledge.

Obedience for Bonhoeffer cannot be extricated from faith, which is the main thrust of *Discipleship* and is the response to costly grace.[92] Obedience is not the requisite demand that derives from an ethical decision but is the responsive faith of the one who is in Christ. This is theological-ontological *Existenz* not predicated on our response to issues of right and wrong; rather, we affirm through obedience that the giver of the commandment is what matters. In the context of *Discipleship*, in following Christ (*nachfolgend*), obedience is therefore imagined not as the activity of one who is subject to the order of rules and regulations but one who is in relationship with the one he follows.

91. *DBWE* 3, 109.
92. *DBWE* 4, 78.

Bonhoeffer's Ethical Method

Freedom is closely connected to obedience for Bonhoeffer, and it is imagined as extrication from the slavery of selfhood—as Bonhoeffer calls it, "the freedom in which the human being belongs wholly to God."[93] Bonhoeffer regards this freedom within the context of obedience because one is freed from the encumbrance of good and evil, the very snares by which the first humans were tempted. One is freed to be obedient.

By the time of *Ethics*, responsibility adopts a prominent role in Bonhoeffer's thinking, though it does not diminish the place of obedience, which maintains a relevant position, bolstered as it is by the introduction of a more creative freedom.[94] Freedom is ana-

93. *DBWE* 3, 109.

94. Here I want to recognize Lovin's essay "Dietrich Bonhoeffer: Responsibility and Restoration," (from *Christian Faith and Public Choices: The Social Ethics of Barth, Brunner, and Bonhoeffer*) in which he makes the assertion that responsibility is a kind of *in extremis* response to unusual ethical dilemmas that in themselves are not meant to uphold the moral dimension of life, but are required in order to reorient and restore obedience to God's commandments. An example of this is characterized in the following sentence: "The venture of responsibility takes place in a situation in which ordinary moral demands provide no guidance" (136). Lovin's Bonhoeffer appears as an act-deontologist (140), which for reasons that cannot be fully developed here I believe is a semantic qualification at best and rather suggests an interpretation of Bonhoeffer as a situation ethicist (cf. Burtness, *Consequences: Morality, Ethics, and the Future*, 65–66). Among my disagreements with Lovin's essay is its lack of engagement with passages specific to the *Ethics* that demonstrate a thoroughgoing connection between responsibility and obedience. For example, Bonhoeffer writes, "Obedience and responsibility are interwoven, so that responsibility does not merely begin where obedience ends, but obedience is rendered in responsibility" (*DBWE* 6, 287). Where Lovin sees responsibility following in a concatenation, and goes so far as to assert that responsibility "falls outside the scope of ethics altogether" (140), I assert Bonhoeffer is clear that in the normal everyday stream of events, responsibility is as much a part of one's vocational existence as it is for valiant men who do great things (see *DBWE* 6, 285–87). Aside from this, Bonhoeffer's only other significant later engagement with the concept of Christian obedience at this time is to correct the misconception that it suggests a blind allegiance and duty, the latter being the very thing Lovin argues is essential to understanding Bonhoeffer's act-deontology (*DBWE* 8, 41). Finally, both responsibility and obedience, along with freedom, have early histories in Bonhoeffer's writings so that their latter usages do not disrupt or transform his theological frame of reference. Thanks to Philip Ziegler for bringing this essay to my attention.

lyzed not only as a pretext for obedience as in Bonhoeffer's earlier work, but is now assimilated as obedience's proper and sustained orientation. On the one hand, the freedom that frees us from the slavery of selfhood *for* obedience is the freedom that likewise keeps us from turning obedience into a form of slavery. "Obedience without freedom is slavery." Likewise, "freedom without obedience is arbitrariness."[95] The emphasis on freedom's role permits a more robust appropriation of obedience, insofar as it leads to Bonhoeffer's concept of responsibility. Freedom, however, does not change its fundamental orientation to the divine. Freedom as a creative activity, rather, asserts itself positively on obedience, for it opens new possibilities for a responsive faith in Christ, primarily in the movement from the sacred to the secular, which may have given Bonhoeffer the theological permission necessary to open the way for the elimination of Hitler. Obedience understood as the dutiful observance of commandments is never simple because too many moving parts exist to distinguish one situation from another and allow for a simple resolution, much less a simple obedience. An obedience, which is called simple, is not nuanced by endless peculiarities, but is oriented to a relationship with Christ that begins with a simple or single (*einfältig*) universal invitation of acceptance. Far from a break with Bonhoeffer's original formulation of obedience, the methodological dimension of responsibility continues to take in the human being as a free subject for whom freedom is only introduced as a more compelling understanding of obedience. The emphasis here is that obedience should not be conceived as a limitation in one's response to Christ but can even be considered creative.

The importance of this creativity is the implication for concrete action that continues as an important methodological dimension in Bonhoeffer's writings. Whether in Barcelona or Fanö, where God is always God "today," to the Berlin lectures where Reimer records how the will of God must be received everyday anew from Christ, to more than a year after his arrest in April 1943, when he was still raising the familiar question: Who is Christ for

---

95. *DBWE* 6, 287.

Bonhoeffer's Ethical Method

us today?, Bonhoeffer's continual awareness of action oriented in Christ remains indivisible from his methodology.[96]

In closing, Bonhoeffer might have said something like the following to explain the application of his Christological ethics: My answer is always in Christ. And my dilemma is always in the world. And since Christ has overcome the world, I am therefore confident where I place my faith.

---

96. Letter to Bethge (April 30, 1944) (*DBWE* 8, 3/137, 362).

— 3 —

Bonhoeffer and the Quest for Peace

ONE OF THE MOST enduring legacies of Bonhoeffer stands in relation to his quest for peace. Was Bonhoeffer an absolute pacifist, a provisional pacifist, or was his theology of peace of an altogether different kind, conditioned by his own unique methodological approach and tied into vicissitudes that developed within the changing tempo of history? With regard to method, we will be occupied with the question of whether Bonhoeffer's pacifism is a starting point *per se* (both provisionally and absolutely) or whether his pacifism is a theme that must be properly situated within this method. While space prevents a comprehensive treatment of every individual passage concerning pacifism in the works of Bonhoeffer, it is my intention to show that Bonhoeffer's pacifism is not synonymous with traditional views of pacifism as nonviolence. To do so, I look at specific and important statements that he made throughout his theological and pastoral career on this matter. Where appropriate, I analyze these passages with particular attention to his methodological approach to ethics.

Three-Part Analysis of Peace

Although pacifism occupies the central position in Bonhoeffer's early resistance activity against Nazi Germany, any characterization of Bonhoeffer as a pacifist without specific qualification presents multiple problems. Those who wish to identify Bonhoeffer as a pacifist face three immediate problems that must be addressed.

The first problem I would characterize as structural. The "worldliness" (*Weltlichkeit*) of Bonhoeffer's ethics, noted in the previous chapter, requires that context, and not principle, provides the shape in which Christ is formed in the world.[1] Apart from the practice of pacifism, (i.e., the way in which one brokers peace to *bring about* the form of Christian peace in the world), Bonhoeffer regards the starting point of peace as relationally ordered. Bonhoeffer writes:

> To be conformed to the image of Jesus Christ is not an ideal of realizing some kind of similarity with Christ which we are asked to attain. It is not we who change ourselves into the image of God. Rather, it is the very image of God, the form of Christ, which seeks to take shape within us ... Our goal is to be shaped into the entire form of the incarnate, the crucified, and the risen one.[2]

The situation described by Bonhoeffer above implies unique and unrepeatable action. One does not seek to mimic Christ; rather one readily anticipates that Christ will be formed within. When peace becomes a methodological approach that is grounded only in its own justification then we cannot "recover the lost image of God." Furthermore, *Weltlichkeit* is limited by its temporality. In other words, an individual's relationship with God is never *then* but always *now*. These structural limitations of worldliness and temporality, which demonstrate Bonhoeffer's appreciation of one's historical circumstances, are consistently present in his ethical approach from his early days and right into *Ethics*.[3] When

---

1. The German term *Weltlichkeit* is rich and can connote the religiously profane, secularism (which for Bonhoeffer is not exempt from theological analysis), or worldliness. These terms may have distinctive connotations in English, but here I simply want to assert Bonhoeffer's ethical concern for the world both in concretion and in taking up form in the reality of the world.

2. *DBWE* 4, 284-85.

3. Even after Barcelona, at which time he speaks about Christian ethics in the case of war as a decision to murder, his affiliation with the ecumenical movement in the World Alliance in search of peace does not cause him to

Bonhoeffer's pacifism is tied to his methodology without regard for temporality and worldliness, pacifism displaces the ethical structure wherein it operates. The result is that *theme* replaces *method*.

The second problem points to an identification of content. Although it is one thing to claim Bonhoeffer was a pacifist, it is quite another thing to examine whether his pacifism, properly defined, requires a sustained engagement of nonviolent activity. For this reason, Green avoids the term "pacifism" entirely, preferring instead "Christian peace ethic." Green writes: "Bonhoeffer's ethic was not an ethic of principles, and 'pacifism' cannot be summarized for him by a principle of nonviolence."[4] Rasmussen notes the difficulty of a purely nonviolent peace when he writes, "Bonhoeffer's self-acclaimed Christian pacifism rarely meets the minimal requirements of any useful definition of pacifism."[5] This raises an important question: Does Bonhoeffer's pacifism take up itself as the means whereby it also accomplishes itself as an end? Further, would such an objection challenge the view of ethical coherence where the road to peace merges with the goal of peace? This question poses problems for those who see Bonhoeffer as an absolute pacifist. Those who define Bonhoeffer's pacifism as a provisional peace must also carefully consider how a provisional orientation toward nonviolence might be affected by the use of violence to achieve peace. Adding complication to this issue is the fact that terms like peace and violence have a firm basis in the world of human affairs. By contrast, when Bonhoeffer sets forth his ethics, he does so with regard to Christ. Subsequently, Bonhoeffer's stance never is an attempt to define the *how* but only the *who*, the ontological rather than the epistemological. To raise the question of *how* his pacifism becomes manifest is to perpetuate the wrong question.

---

reject his contextual approach. See *NRS* 161–63 (cf. *DBWE* 6, 99).

4. See *DBWE* 10, 10.

5. Rasmussen, *Dietrich Bonhoeffer: Reality and Resistance*, 96 (cf. Clifford J. Green, "Pacifism and Tyrannicide," 32–33). Green notes that Bonhoeffer rarely used the word "pacifist" or "pacifism."

The third problem, closely tied to the first, is representative of the Socratic problem of the pious.[6] When any ethical response is seized upon as the universal, the universal itself is no longer in need of justification because it *is its own* justification. The consequence of such a view is that Christ need not be the ground of one's ethical response since it is enough justification that the universal is coherent. Such a situation is problematic for Bonhoeffer who would insist that ethical responses must originate with Christ if they are to be authentic. Yet, any ethic that is claimed to derive from a supernatural origin will be subject to skepticism.[7] A pacifism wholly grounded in the world, Bonhoeffer would claim, is still subject to Christ, authentic even in its rejection of its origin. Indeed, Christocentric ethical responses *do* become indistinguishable from responses made by those outside of Christ, and Bonhoeffer is clear that ethics is not the unique treasure trove of the Christian witness. Peace, for example, cannot be a universal and self-evident reality if each individual is left to discover it. The "self-evident" nature of peace (a claim Bonhoeffer will come to make by 1932) is evident *only* in relationship to Christ.[8] Bonhoeffer raises another problem: making the ethical the absolute means that "only the isolated individual is considered ethically relevant" and easily delineates between standards of good and evil.[9] The reality of this supposed isolated individual becomes as absolute as the commandment he holds. It should be noted that this is close to, but not the same as, Kierkegaard's notion of the ethical universal, which attempts to supplant concrete humanity so that a certain transgression of the ethical needs to occur before such humans can make authentic ethical determinations.[10] In *Sanctorum Communio*, Bonhoeffer avoids this trap by expressing the necessity of

---

6. In the *Euthyphro* dialogue, Socrates poses the question of whether the pious is loved by the gods because it is pious, or is it pious because it is loved by the gods? (Plato, *Euthyphro*, § 10a).

7. Burtness, *Consequences*, 13.

8. Bethge, *Dietrich Bonhoeffer: A Biography*, 209.

9. *DBWE* 6, 218.

10. See p. 11.

the individual's relationship to the Other. He writes further on the topic in later works, stating the same objection but with specific attention paid to Christ who takes on himself humanity. The emphasis is on the ethical rather than soteriological dimension.[11]

The importance of this analysis is in establishing that Bonhoeffer's reflections on peace are not at all uniform, are not methodologically essential, and are always subsumed by the necessity of relationship in Christ. By extension, the relationship between peace and violence is deconstructed as themes rather than starting points in ethical decision making. Here, our concern in this chapter will remain with the way pacifism functions as a theme within Bonhoeffer's methodology. Whether pacifism requires the elimination of all violence or includes violence as a means to an end is of secondary importance because the more important concern is how his method operates—a method that may take in any number of definitions of pacifism at different times. At the same time, I will investigate the way in which absolute and provisional pacifism might be applied, and in doing so, expose their insufficiencies that preclude a proper orientation to the peace that begins with and remains in Christ.

Early Tendencies Toward Peace

From his early writings in Barcelona, Bonhoeffer's definition of peace can be reconstructed in three specific senses. The first can be inferred by the outcome that arose for *lack of* peace due to Germany's role in World War I. Of the 144 provisions in the Treaty of Versailles, 140 were imposed to punish Germany. The general feeling among Germans was that the harsh stipulations imposed by the treaty created impossible conditions and so drew Germany into a climate of societal unrest. As Robertson points out, "There was a widespread belief that the victorious Allies intended to reduce Germany to a non-entity in Europe, and that their main

---

11. Ibid., 231.

instrument was the iniquitous and unjust Versailles Treaty."[12] This point is supported by Staats who notes that Bonhoeffer's "call to peace among the nations is always accompanied by apologetic-patriotic recollections about Germany's fate in World War I and by a sharp rejection of the Versailles treaty, with its ascription of guilt solely to Germany."[13] With a second defeat looming by the late '30s and early '40s, more sanctions and harsher punishments were once again feared. Robertson claims that during his time as a conspirator, Bonhoeffer too pondered "whether the present resistance movement could set up another regime in Germany and still survive."[14] Concern that all of Germany would be treated indiscriminately despite pockets of resistance to Hitler was not Bonhoeffer's alone. At a gathering of Nazi officials in Munich on November 8, 1938, *Reichsführer-SS* Heinrich Himmler predicted that failure on the part of Germany would result in the persecution of all Germans, regardless of whether or not one claimed the Nazis: "You mark my words, in the decisive battle to come, if we are defeated we will be given no quarter, they will be allowed to starve to death or butchered. That will be the fate of every man, whether he be an enthusiastic supporter or not, it will be enough that German is his mother tongue."[15]

When Bonhoeffer delivered his first lecture to the congregation in Barcelona, he began with a vivid reminder of the distress of the German people during the Great War. Calling this a time of "unprecedented crisis," Bonhoeffer recollected the ways in which life had changed. In these recollections, Bonhoeffer's interest in the recent past implies that peace had not been realized. True peace was denied to the German people, he declared, for peace

12. Robertson, *The Shame and the Sacrifice*, 86.
13. *DBWE* 10, 609.
14. Robertson, *The Shame and the Sacrifice*, 204.
15. I use MacDonogh's translation from his book *1938: Hitler's Gamble*, 219. (Microfilm of Himmler's speech, November 8, 1938, RFSS/T-175, 90/2612546, The National Archives and Records Service, General Services Administration, Washington: 1961). A similar statement is made by Joseph Goebbels on December 13, 1941, in reference to a speech given by Hitler. Thanks to Peter C. Hoffmann for pointing this out.

is only possible where there is a mutual respect.[16] This feeling of international injustice toward Germany is never fully reconciled in his reflections. Bonhoeffer's later rejection of an unconditional surrender by 1942 appears situated in his concern against harsh repercussions and his concern that a post-war Germany would be subject to the whims of disinterested victors who would install sanctions to their benefit.[17] Bonhoeffer felt so strongly on this issue that he could even consider siding with the Socialists if it was clear that the Allies had no interest in a post-war preservation of those elements in Germany that were opposed to Hitler.[18] A general feeling that the realization of peace depended upon conditional criteria is clear in a secret memorandum created by the Bishop of Chichester, George K. A. Bell, which was based upon his conversations with Bonhoeffer.[19] German resistance historian Peter C. Hoffmann noted that if the Allies would not negotiate with the opposition to install and recognize a new government, the resistance itself would be forced to "fight to the bitter end."[20]

In spite of this, there was a sense in the religious sentiment of the day that the situation facing Germany was a result of the wrath of God. In 1941, the popular and outspoken Roman Catholic bishop Clemens August Count von Galen, speaking to his congregation in Münster, declared:

> I hope there is still time, but then indeed it is high time: That we may realise, in this our day, the things that belong unto our peace! That we may realise what alone can save us, can preserve us from the divine judgment: that we should take the divine commandments as the guiding rule of our lives and act in sober earnest according to the words, "Rather die than sin." That in prayer and sincere

---

16. A deleted addition in another sermon at this time speaks to the condition of mutual peace: "But with regard to both human beings and God, the path to peace means–forgiveness. Only a marriage, a friendship, built on mutual forgiveness can have peace." (*DBWE* 10, 3/18, 549, n. 15.)
17. Kelly and Nelson, *Testament to Freedom*, 38.
18. Robertson, *The Shame and the Sacrifice*, 204.
19. *DBWE* 16, 1/181, 319–24.
20. Hoffmann, *History of the German Resistance: 1933–1945*, 221.

penitence we should beg that God's forgiveness and mercy may descend upon us, upon our city, our country and our beloved German people.[21]

Bonhoeffer never went so far as to place complete blame on Germany's enemies for the hardships suffered. When he recalls the Great War, he interprets the past thoughtfully, sensitive to its theological meaning, which he too concludes is the divine judgment of God against German pride. This theme followed him through his career. Sitting in a cell in 1943, his words sound very much like those of his Barcelona years as he reflects on the judgment of God now facing his nation once again: *"Darum müssen wir das, was wir erleben, wirklich in uns bewahren, verarbeiten, fruchtbar werden lassen und es nicht von uns abschütteln. Noch nie haben wir den zornigen Gott so handgreiflich zu spüren bekommen, und das ist Gnade."*[22]

Growing up in the shadow of the Great War helped Bonhoeffer think soberly about peace. Bonhoeffer, as he struggles to communicate his thoughts on peace to his congregation in Barcelona, begins the process of forgiveness and reconciliation with a world that did not know or perhaps care that it was being reconciled.

Left behind in Bonhoeffer's writings during this time are passages that express the beginnings of his reflections on peace. These reflections are particularly important because the young pastor was speaking to an audience composed primarily of German expatriates who were desperate for someone like Bonhoeffer to reconnect them to their homeland. What is striking is the way in which Christian love underscores his interest in peace. The following example could have been written at any time in his career: "Judging destroys every community. Loving, pardoning, interceding, that alone builds it up. No marriage, no friendship endures without this most profound, forgiving, nonjudgmental love. No rearing of youth can succeed unless we make ourselves equal in

---

21. Griech-Polelle, *Bishop von Galen*, 195.

22. "Therefore, we must really preserve what we experience, process it, let it become fruitful and not shake it off. We have never had to feel the angry God so violently, and that is grace" (my translation). (*DBW* 8:2/79, 211).

love . . . Neither can there be any national community [*Volksgemeinschaft*] as long as people seek to judge."²³

That Bonhoeffer projects the need for equality first to his people rather than formally to outsiders suggests that he knows any overture of peace must first begin internally, with the healing process in Germany. The word *Volksgemeinschaft* here is directed at Germany with a distinctive prohibition in which judging refers to particular claims being made among Germans.²⁴

Yet shortly afterward, Bonhoeffer preaches on 1 Corinthians 12:27, 26. Here, he extends the meaning of the community to its broadest sense: the people of God. More specifically a community of people that is, "not Germany and not France and not America, but a people extending over the entire world, whose members can be found here and there and everywhere . . . This is the people of God; this is the church of Christ."²⁵ The background of this sermon is noteworthy: By July 1928, Bonhoeffer had become well liked in the community at Barcelona and regularly made it a point to interact with the Spanish people. To speak now only of Germany, one would imagine, would be to betray these broader sensitivities.²⁶ It is not unreasonable then to believe that the seeds of ecumenism,

---

23. *DBWE* 10, 3/6, 499.

24. Verhey notes that "in 1926, the government's press agency, after defining the *Volksgemeinschaft* as the recognition of a common bond, a common fate, and a healthy nationalism, claimed that 'the reawakening and growth again of Germany depends upon the unity of the empire and the whole German people.'" The idea had not yet been radicalized for its more oppressive racial overtones (see *The Spirit of 1914*, 216). Nolzen proposes that the radicalization of the term as a racial concept only comes after 1933 (see *Germany and the Second World War*, 201). Bonhoeffer is most likely concerned with cultural division at his time, witnessed in competing ideologies and the fracturing of political parties, all of which lent itself to the rise of class consciousness (see Bendersky, *History of Nazi Germany: 1919–1945*, 133).

25. *DBWE* 10, 3/8, 507.

26. Bonhoeffer's own concern for those of differing ethnicities and beliefs remains a consistent theme. From his viewing of *All Quiet on the Western Front* in New York with Jean Lasserre to his concern that his Russian companion and atheist Wasily Wasiliew Kokorin would be offended by an impromptu Christian service immediately prior to their executions (Bethge, *Dietrich Bonhoeffer: A Biography*, 926).

and the cause for peace that would later become so important during his New York years, germinated first in the soil of Spain.[27] Here also, Bonhoeffer extends the concept of reconciliation beyond the *Volk* to the "other person." The church could only be the church when it acted as Christ for others. The Christ who reconciles himself to the world could be practically tested on Spanish soil during those years through Bonhoeffer's work in a congregation that at times featured both Germans and Spaniards. In a sermon on 1 John 2:17 in August 1928, Bonhoeffer speaks of the church as being that which recognizes eternity by embracing this life, a revelation only possible when one does the will of God—actions that included, among other things, being "peace-loving and compassionate."[28]

In a sermon dated February 3, 1929, which was to be his last in Barcelona, Bonhoeffer introduces a third sense in which peace must be defined. Here, commenting on Philippians 4:7, Bonhoeffer distinguishes between the peace of God and peace that originates in the world. He encourages his congregation to find rest in the former.[29] The thinking here differs only slightly from his sermon on 1 Corinthians 12:27, 26 in that peace is now directly mentioned and it is Christ who offers his peace in which we must find rest. "With elementary force, however, the call for peace again and again breaks out among humanity, first powerfully and mightily in the ancient prophets, and now most recently again in the longing for world peace everywhere. But as beautiful and well-intentioned as all these hopes are, they fail to recognize that the peace we need is the peace that comes down to us from eternity, the peace of God with humanity, with every individual among us."[30]

Peace is universal. It resuscitates in humanity; and yet where God is not the ground of this intention, peace is insufficient to

---

27. Further evidence of a developing affinity for foreigners comes in his comment in which he questions whether Barth had ever spent any time abroad, implying that Barth's theology remained very German (*DBWE* 10, 1/5, 64).

28. *DBWE* 10, 3/11, 520.

29. Ibid., 3/18, 548.

30. Ibid.

bring about real change. Peace must be grounded in God. Here, Bonhoeffer's Christological ethic, though arguably nascent, is manifesting. Furthermore, those of us who find only semblances of peace and do not find peace in God are still "without peace" (*friedlos*), a term Bonhoeffer uses on multiple occasions in this sermon.[31]

Bonhoeffer goes on to express how transitory expressions of peace are symbols that reflect the intransitory expression of peace. Admittedly, Bonhoeffer's analysis here creates more questions than answers. There is no clarification on how a symbol and a semblance meaningfully differ in this context.[32] A possible hint to his meaning comes from Green who points out that his use of the concepts of "transitory" and "intransitory" derives from a passage in Johann Wolfgang von Goethe's *Faust*.[33] If this is true, then it is possible that Bonhoeffer is responding to Plato *and* Nietzsche, the latter whom in *Thus Spoke Zarathustra* appears also to be alluding

---

31. Green asserts the usual meaning of *friedlos* used in this sermon is "outcast" (*Friedlosigkeit*, lit. "without peace"), which has a medieval Germanic legal connotation for a person who commits a particularly heinous crime and as a result is alienated from society. I would suggest that this is only one reading because the concept is not without debate, particularly with regard to types of crime and their consequential outcomes for the individual's status in the community (see Lupoi, *Origins of the European Legal Order*, 369). If Green's interpretation of *friedlos* is correct, it sets the argument in one direction, which creates a radical alienation from God. In my opinion, *friedlos* cannot imply radical, existential alienation so long as humanity maintains, in Bonhoeffer's account, a desire for peace despite its fallen condition (the radicality with which Barth touches this question does not approach the kind of moderate position found in Bonhoeffer's Lutheran theological tradition). Bonhoeffer's notion that Germany has been deprived of peace remains structured in the hope of peace so long as there is reconciliation, which begins in Germany's own ability to accept responsibility.

32. *DBWE* 10, 3/18, 548.

33. Bonhoeffer was acquainted with Tillich who was known for his interpretation of symbols and the existential reality to which they pointed. However, his three-volume work *Systematic Theology* (1951–1963) in which this is worked out comes years later.

to *Faust*.[34] Frances Nesbitt Oppel has pointed out that in the section "On the Blissful Islands":

> The text plays with the ending of Goethe's poem *Faust*, where Faust's soul is saved from the devil and "drawn upward" to heaven by the love of a pure woman, as the mystical chorus eulogizes the "intransitory" and the "eternal feminine" that draw us ever upward. The "eternal feminine" in Zarathustra is the "eternal return," which draws us ever downward,to the earth, to time, to the transitory.[35]

One might say that Bonhoeffer rejects both a Platonic view that de-emphasizes the position of the world as an imperfect reflection of the eternal and Nietzsche for his emphasis on the unflinching dominion of the transitory, which essentially diminishes the reality of God. Bonhoeffer instead seeks confluence between the eternal and the real. Bonhoeffer's mention of peace in the passages above is hardly trivial, nor is it a passing thought. He is concerned with peace as a manifestation in the believer's life, but not as an approach to ethics or methodological starting point for fear that it risks losing God for an experience of God.

"Discovering" Pacifism in New York

Bonhoeffer's interstitial period in Berlin yields relatively little in the way of strong stands on the issue of peace. By contrast, Bonhoeffer's experiences in New York are often considered to have laid the groundwork for his pacifism. This period in New York was likely influenced by Jean Lasserre, a Frenchman and fellow seminarian

---

34. Venting his own frustration and veiled criticism of Plato, Nietzsche writes, "*Gotte ist ein Gedanke, der macht alles Gerade krumm und Alles, was steht, drehend. Wie? Die Zeit wäre hinweg, und alles Vergängliche nur Lüge?*" "God is an idea that makes everything straight crooked and sets everything stationary spinning. What? Are we to eliminate time and call all transitory things a mere lie?" (Nietzsche, *Thus Spoke Zarathustra (Selections), Also Sprach Zarathustra (Auswahl): A Dual-Language Book*, 80–81).

35. Oppel, *Nietzsche on Gender: Beyond Man and Woman*, 163.

at Union Theological Seminary, who had adopted a lasting interest in the question of peace and made active inroads to affect peaceful change.[36]

Bonhoeffer made the trip to New York in September 1930 on a study grant at Union Theological Seminary. It should be noted that prior to his trip to New York and meeting Jean Lasserre, Bonhoeffer composed a text on "War" that he intended to be read while he was in the United States. It seems that Bonhoeffer understood his own unofficial role as an ambassador of good will for his nation, and that it would be his task to heal and correct perspectival rifts. Bonhoeffer's preparation paid off. Not only did he find himself lecturing on the war (in his words "frequently")[37] but in return he was encouraged by American academics who expressed interest in the future of Germany.[38]

This encouragement no doubt boosted his confidence in his relationships with non-Germans. His noteworthy desire for companionship among foreigners and even interest in other religious traditions was evident early in Bonhoeffer's life. Examples include his excursions to Libya, where he spoke fondly of the Arab population, and then Italy, and Spain, followed by an anticipated trip to India. All provide evidence that his friendships at Union, which included time spent with the African American Frank Fisher, the Frenchman Lasserre, the American Paul Lehmann, and the Swiss student Erwin Sutz, had an international flavor. In fashion similar to his experiences in Barcelona where he opted for housing among the locals, and also expressed earlier in his interest for intimacy with Italians in Rome, Bonhoeffer did his best to acclimate to life in the United States. "I completely stayed away from the German club

---

36. Lasserre's own influence on Bonhoeffer's pacifism is debated. Green defends this connection (*DBWE* 10, 26–27). Kelly and Godsey note the majority view (*DBWE* 4, 14); Rasmussen notes Bonhoeffer's concerns for peace prior to Lasserre. (*Dietrich Bonhoeffer: Reality and Resistance*, 100, n. 15). Ironically, neither Lasserre nor Lasserre's view of pacifism is mentioned by Bonhoeffer from prison.

37. *DBWE* 10, 1/181, 319.

38. "Much is said here about the political situation in Germany, and with great sympathy, particularly in academic circles." (Ibid., 1/53, 271).

life," he said, indicating also that he "did not spend much time in the German churches."[39] Bonhoeffer spoke fondly of the existence of an international house at Union.[40] Furthermore, after being shut out of services on Easter Sunday for the reason of not procuring reserved seating soon enough, he ventured to hear the preaching of the popular rabbi Stephen Wise.[41] Far from discovering ecumenism in America, Staats writes, "In America, he thus continues and strengthens the developments of ecumenical understanding of the church on which he first embarked in Barcelona."[42] What can be said about New York is that for the first time Bonhoeffer experiences a fruitful period of intellectual reciprocity in which he encounters others who were serious about peace. By way of the Frenchman Lasserre, the possibility of peace broke through its theoretical barriers. Bonhoeffer could look at his French "enemy," the one whose country he blamed for creating impossible stipulations against his own, and call him friend. Moving about with Lasserre, in particular during their trip to Mexico in May 1931 to deliver lectures on peace, allowed Bonhoeffer to see the effect of their partnership as a concrete reality.[43]

Yet other writing from that time reveals Bonhoeffer had not pledged himself to absolute pacifism. For example, he revels in the even-handedness of the war account given by Robert C. Sheriff in *Journey's End*, which was part of his coursework at Union in a class called Ethical Viewpoints in Modern Literature. The review he gives minds an attitude of neutrality: "The most impressive of

39. Ibid., 1/182, 321.
40. Ibid., 1/141, 251–52.
41. Ibid., 1/169, 295.
42. Ibid., 630.
43. Tödt notes that seeing a Frenchman and German together "deeply impressed the hundreds of listeners." (*Authentic Faith*, 119); Lasserre himself states in an interview about their time in South America: "that was so unusual because it seemed to them that French and German had always been at war with one another and that it was unbelievable that they would be both on the same panel and still more speak of peace together, though France and Germany had given the impression that the main goal in life was to fight against each other" (Boehlke and Drake, *Dietrich Bonhoeffer: Memories and Perspectives*).

all war books I read has been for me *Journey's End*. Here is no tendency neither in a pacifistic nor in an idealistic-patriotic way, nor is it only a description of events. It is written out of the concrete situation in its immense earnestness."[44] Nevertheless, the call to peace sounds off strongly in other places of Bonhoeffer's work. In his previously composed text on war, presumably read to multiple congregations, Bonhoeffer considers it an unthinkable act that a Christian brother should take up arms against his brother.[45] The quote itself is also preserved in another version of this address and is notable for its sermon-like quality.[46]

Growing in Peace

Bonhoeffer's writings after his return to Germany in 1931 provide some of his most significant statements on peace. In a letter from August 1931, Bonhoeffer informs Lehmann about a catechism he has prepared in collaboration with Franz Hildebrandt that prominently features the concept of discipleship and the Sermon on the Mount.[47] Perhaps most important in this development, and what Green calls "the kernel of the book *Discipleship*," is the lecture Bonhoeffer delivered in late 1932 for the ecumenical working group of the German Christian Student Association.[48] This lecture is almost

44. *DBWE* 10, 11.1, 420.

45. Ibid., 2/9, 417.

46. Rasmussen cites an interview with Otto Dudzus, a former student of Bonhoeffer, whose comments about Bonhoeffer's message at Fanö (1934) suggest a certain carefulness when distinguishing between emphasis on pacifistic concrete action by the church and a call to a general attitude of pacifism. (*Dietrich Bonhoeffer: Reality and Resistance*, 105); Dudzus makes it clear that pacifistic concrete action is not something less than pacifism: "This passionate call to a world Church which feels itself responsible for peace was for Bonhoeffer not an isolated affair which was broken off because it obviously found no echo. He stuck to this responsibility throughout all the complications and confusions, including his personal 'change' from pacifist to an active resistance fighter." Dudzus believes that peace for Bonhoeffer was not synonymous with nonviolence (Dudzus "Arresting the Wheel," 90).

47. *DBW* 17:11/1/8a.

48. It was previously and erroneously identified as the Berlin Branch of

always considered to be a touchstone for those who see Bonhoeffer's move to pacifism in this era. It is therefore important to look closely at this lecture to determine what Bonhoeffer is saying. Bonhoeffer begins by offering concessions: "It is true that Christ has not given us specific rules for our conduct... However, this does not mean that the gospel of Jesus Christ does not give a clear answer to the problems that confront us."[49]

In an important section from the lecture on who receives peace, Bonhoeffer interprets Jesus' statement from Matthew 10:34: "I have not come to bring peace, but a sword." Bonhoeffer notes that this peace is a gift "given to us with Christ." Peace is not commanded but is primarily an orientation conceived first in Christ's love for humanity and then commanded to every person for whom it must also be their orientation. Furthermore, Bonhoeffer notes this commandment to peace is beyond good and evil. The commandment does not require anyone to frustrate his or her thinking over sophistications of right and wrong. The "clear answer" is none other than relationship in Christ.

Following this, Bonhoeffer goes on to assert that "peace can never consist in reconciling the gospel with religious worldviews." Instead true peace cuts through like a sword, dividing itself from the worldly form of peace. Bonhoeffer's earlier discussion about the problem of peace in the world against the peace that comes from God, a theme that echoes Barcelona, helps locate this claim as a dichotomy that continued in his writings. The idea that a uniform notion of peace exists is akin to "false doctrine." The peace of the gospel originates from the relationship an individual experiences in Christ. The peace that comes from religious worldviews is one of law and order. Bonhoeffer asserts that Matthew 10:34 is not about the commandment *to* peace but reconciliation. Only where reconciliation occurs is relationship possible. For as long as there is no repentance, there can be no peace. There cannot be peace at all costs as long as the "defiant sinner" exists. It is important to note, however, that Bonhoeffer rejects a religious and worldly

---

the Student Christian Movement in *DBWE* 10, 34.

49. *DBWE* 12, 2/6, 259.

peace not because the sinner alone persists but because the sinner by virtue of being a sinner ignores the relational dimension of obedience in Christ. For Bonhoeffer, peace outside of Christ is already predetermined in its character and composition because it is substantiated by ideal characteristics (nonviolence, security, toleration, and harmony). This means that even while addressing the execution of peace in the world, peace is removed from the concrete circumstances of that world. Bonhoeffer notes: "It was not Christ's concern to change the conditions he found in this world in order to bring about security, peace, and quiet. Much less should we think that we can do away with outward sins and the horrors of war through political treatises. As long as the world is free of God, there will be wars."[50]

The peace of the world is antithetical to the peace of God. The job of the peacemaker is then not to prevent war but to pray for one's enemy. We find this message in Barcelona, in which one must pray for the very person he is attempting to kill in battle, and notably this message continues into *Discipleship*. It is interesting, however, that the activity of prayer loses its centrality for Bonhoeffer as he moves deeper into the conspiracy, especially during his work on *Ethics*. Prayer, as grasping the will of God, is replaced by Christ's grasping of the world of which we are already a part. "Christ in the world" takes the place of a summons of Christ through prayer.

With regard to Bonhoeffer's methodology, it is notable here that the greatest good is not peace but love. Peace is directed by love. One is not called to peace, but one has peace and consequently makes peace when touched by the love of God.[51] Out of this situation, peace becomes significant, and not the other way around. Peace is not the ground of our ethics because it is subject

---

50. Ibid. While he includes peace and security separately here, it should be noted that around this same time in Fanö (1934), Bonhoeffer considers security a false representation of peace, calling peace a risk and something that must be dared, while security has just the opposite effect.

51. Bonhoeffer, *Discipleship*, 108, 141, 151–152. The premise of those conversations in *Discipleship* concerning one's attitude of peace towards one's enemies is the accomplishment of peace through love, which for Bonhoeffer is an existential condition a priori to one's outward motivations and actions.

to confusion outside of Christ. Love interprets the commandments, and the commandments are expressions of love, not right and wrong. All of this then presses the question of a momentous turn to peace experienced by Bonhoeffer in the early 1930s, the discussion of which is found in a personal letter written in 1936 to Elizabeth Zinn.[52] The year 1936, of course, is marked by the rise of Hitler to the Chancellery. Bonhoeffer calls this a crisis. The important section of this letter reads as follows: "I suddenly saw the Christian pacifism that I had recently passionately opposed as self-evident—during the defense of my dissertation, where Gerhard [Jacobi] was also present. And so it went on, step by step. I no longer saw or thought anything else."[53]

Looking back, if we read Bonhoeffer here to mean that peace had been placed irreconcilably outside the realm of appropriate responses so that it was only during this event that peace became the *summum bonum* of the Christian witness, how are we now to prosecute the details or analyze the information we have already examined?

This turn is often attached to Bonhoeffer's own words that come a few sentences earlier in this letter. It is that passage where he describes experiencing a "great liberation." Upon closer inspection, however, the liberation Bonhoeffer experiences was not because he had rethought pacifism in a distinctively Christian way but rather that he *became* a Christian because he started approaching the Bible, and in particular the Sermon on the Mount, with new eyes. Aligned to this new perspective, he understood God's call to community, where before he had admittedly been lord over his own life. The emphasis at first is ironic considering the subject matter of *Sanctorum Communio*. The fight against Christian pacifism, however, is not an admission to some former militaristic attitude—in fact his letter has nothing to do with this tension—but,

---

52. Green, "Pacifism and Tyrannicide," 32. Green, too, contends that Bonhoeffer's time in Barcelona demonstrates that he is "not entirely free" from *völkische* theology and points to his lecture on Christian ethics (cf. *DBWE* 10, 2/3, 369–74). Moses writes that this letter included his confession to "love one's enemies." *Reluctant Revolutionary*, 134.

53. Bethge, *Dietrich Bonhoeffer: A Biography*, 205.

in the spirit of personal letter writing, is rather a spiritual admission about letting go of his own life in order to allow the peace of Christ's full reign. In my opinion, Bonhoeffer's liberation is best read as a move to personal submission, a fact which should not be confused with an anachronistic evangelical concept of born-again soteriology, as if prior to 1936, Bonhoeffer only appealed to his Christianity in vain.

It should be noted that the authoritative nature of Christ was hardly a foreign concept to Bonhoeffer while in Barcelona. Bonhoeffer's sermon on 1 Corinthians 12:27, 26 reminds how all peoples are bound to Christ such that the church is not compelled by the interests of any one state. Again with regard to the turn Bonhoeffer experienced in his life, we are left to grapple with what appear to be different events that are expressed in autobiographical recollections. In a letter from April 22, 1944, Bonhoeffer writes: "I don't think I've ever changed very much, except perhaps at the time of my first impressions abroad, and under the first conscious influence of Papa's personality. It was then that a turning away from the phraseological to the real ensued."[54] Contrary to Hans Christoph von Hase's assertion that in this letter Bonhoeffer is speaking of the years between Barcelona and New York, Bonhoeffer's *first* impressions would have to have been during his travels to Italy, which preceded Barcelona.[55] Here in Italy, he recalls an important intellectual transformation and confesses that this was the first time he discovered what it meant to be the church. Yet this experience bears no direct relation with a change to pacifism. Rather, testimony about the time he spent in Italy infers a connection to work he begins shortly after on the sociality of the church in *Sanctorum Communio*.[56]

---

54. *DBWE* 8, 3/135, 358.

55. *DBWE* 10, 591.

56. Further evidence that Bonhoeffer's letter is pointing to his experiences in Italy is driven by Hase's assertion that Bonhoeffer's goal in becoming a theologian, a decision he claims Bonhoeffer makes at the age of 14, was in concern for peace. If this is true, then peace must have played an important role in his Christian witness prior to its nurturing at Union Theological Seminary in the early 1930s and making the claim debatable that Bonhoeffer is here referring to his time spent in New York. (Ibid., 595).

BONHOEFFER AND THE QUEST FOR PEACE

Peace and the Ecumenical Movement

The potential for practical opportunities to exercise his ecumenical thinking proved to be only a matter of time for the cause of peace. Even before Bonhoeffer held any official role in the church, he was asked by his cousin Hase whether he had abandoned Germany theology to become an ecumenist.[57]

Bonhoeffer's interest in creating relationships within the global church community found initial expression in his elected role as youth co-secretary for Germany and Europe through the World Alliance for Promoting International Friendship through the Churches. In September 1931, Bonhoeffer attended a four-day conference in Cambridge. The excitement and rush of being a part of something that potentially had the power to create real change must have moved Bonhoeffer deeply. Real issues were discussed with political implications, among those being the League of Nations Charter articles that restricted the arming of signing nations.

Rasmussen has characterized Bonhoeffer's lectures during this time as the best evidence that Bonhoeffer was moving further away from the stances in Barcelona that had left for him the question of a justifiable war all but closed.[58] This marked change of course is accompanied by some of the strongest condemnations of war he had given to date. These are found in a lecture Bonhoeffer delivered at Gland, Switzerland, in 1932 and then in a sermon delivered at Fanö, Denmark, in 1934. The question of whether or not Bonhoeffer was becoming the absolute pacifist that he is largely remembered to be during these years is summed up by Kelly and Godsey:

> So pronounced was the change from 'realist' to pacifist that few statements in support of the peace movement, even today, can match the fire and passion of Bonhoeffer's Berlin lecture 'Christ and Peace'; his denunciation of the idolatry of national security at the ecumenical conference in Gland, Switzerland, in August 1932; his disturbing challenge to the churches to be advocates for

---

57. Letter from November 30, 1930 (Ibid., 1/143, 253).
58. Rasmussen, *Dietrich Bonhoeffer: Reality and Resistance*, 101.

peace in a sermon, 'The Church and the Peoples of the World,' at the ecumenical gathering in Fanö, Denmark, in September 1934.[59]

A further statement on the need for peace, recalls Bethge, "is the most unequivocal and emphatic of his statements on peace that we possess."[60] As his work in the ecumenical movement was at its height, and as he was enjoying the support of his colleagues, Bonhoeffer explained how the ecumenical church is the church of God that transcends the boundaries of national loyalty.

> Peace on earth is not a problem, but a commandment given at Christ's coming. There are two ways of reacting to this command from God: the unconditional, blind obedience of action, or the hypocritical question of the Serpent: "Yea, hath God said . . ?" This question is the mortal enemy of obedience, and therefore the mortal enemy of all real peace. "Has God not said? Has God not understood human nature well enough to know that wars must occur in this world, like laws of nature? Must God not have meant that we should talk about peace, to be sure, but that it is not to be literally translated into action? Must God not really have said that we should work for peace, of course, but also make ready tanks and poison gas for security?" And then perhaps the most serious question: "Did God say you should not protect your own people? Did God say you should leave your own prey to the enemy?" No, God did not say all that. What he has said is that here shall be peace among men—that we shall obey him without further question, that is what he means. He who questions the commandment of God before obeying has already denied him.[61]

It is therefore notable that despite the very strong language here, Robertson asserts that Bonhoeffer was making a "call to peace, but not to pacifism."[62] However, it is a form of pacifism,

59. *DBWE* 4, 14.
60. Bethge, *Dietrich Bonhoeffer: A Biography*, 388.
61. *NRS*, 289–90.
62. Ibid., 289. Bethge notes that Bonhoeffer was not concerned with

notes Jørgen Glenthøj, that can only be understood from within Bonhoeffer's own Lutheran tradition. "*Bonhoeffer wurde etwas im Jahre 1932 Pazifist, Friedenstifter, aber ein lutherischer Pazifist.*" Glenthøj goes on to say that while this understanding is found in the distinctive Lutheran understanding of God's activity in church and the state, Bonhoeffer was also a product of social awareness and generational concerns for peace.[63] Interestingly, Lasserre, whose pacifism has been regarding as influencing Bonhoeffer's young theological career, discussed the Fanö speech in an interview, responding that Bonhoeffer's point could be summarized as follows: "*Now* we shall not go to war. We must find another way to serve our problems."[64] The contextualism of this quote is not lost on Rasmussen, either. Commenting on Bonhoeffer's statement that "Today God's command for us is the order of international peace,"[65] he notes the intentional usage of the word "today," which for Rasmussen frames Bonhoeffer's persistent contextualism and "underlines Bonhoeffer's continuing conviction about the concrete *now* of Christ's command."[66]

Here, Bonhoeffer's ethical method underpins his statements on peace. First, the commandment of God is always the concrete word of God to humanity. As a concrete manifestation, the commandment of peace is also the commandment of God for us *today*. Nevertheless, it is a spiritual peace because it is wrapped up in our own understanding of our orientation to God. It is relational because God reconciles us to himself, so that also "there shall be peace among men." Yet still, when we understand this as God's commandment, we are not permitted to respond abstractly

---

open-ended questions but "with the direct demand that certain decisions be risked" (*Dietrich Bonhoeffer: A Biography*, 388).

63. "*Dietrich Bonhoeffer gehörte einer Generation an, der in der Jugendzeit unauslöschlich in die Erinnerung gebrannt worden war, was Kreig bedeutet*" (Glenthøj, "*Dietrich Bonhoeffers Weg vom Pazifismus zum politischen Widerstand*," 49).

64. Boehlke and Drake, *Dietrich Bonhoeffer: Memories and Perspectives*. Italics are my emphasis.

65. *NRS*, 167.

66. Rasmussen, *Dietrich Bonhoeffer: Reality and Resistance*, 105.

because God's peace is of the kind that can only be understood here and now.

This philosophical realism allows Bonhoeffer to negotiate the concept of peace between two poles: God's commandment for those who are "working for peace," which has not yet attained, and God's peace expressed as a reality that has not yet attained in the world, but is *nevertheless* real because God commands "peace among men."

It is also important to note that the ethical question raised by the serpent (see chapter 2) is the fulcrum upon which the creation story rests. It is no coincidence the image of the serpent finds itself here because the timing of this sermon approximates the writing of *Creation and Fall* where Bonhoeffer discusses sin through the Genesis story. The figures of Adam and Eve echo in the warning from his 1934 Fanö address: "He who questions the commandment of God before obeying has already denied Him."

Discipleship

Arguably Bonhoeffer's best known work, *Discipleship*, receives ample attention regarding its views on peace.[67] Written between 1934 and 1935, though conceived in 1932, *Discipleship* builds on earlier formulations in Bonhoeffer's sermons and interactions, as Kelly and Godsey have noted.[68] On the question of pacifism, the book is regularly interpreted as a manifesto on the subject. Mark Devine, for example, considers the statements on peace found in it to be "almost absolutist pronouncements."[69] Nonacademic in its tone, however, it is not considered to be on the level of his more scholarly works, even though the relationship between the concept of discipleship and ethics was subject matter being discussed in scholarly Protestant circles during the same period. In 1929, for

---

67. Originally published as *The Cost of Discipleship* in English, *DBWE* 4 restores the more accurate translation of the German word *Nachfolge* to *Discipleship*.

68. *DBWE* 4, 2.

69. Devine, *Bonhoeffer Speaks Today*, 137.

example, Arvid Runestam made a general observation about the place of discipleship in Protestantism, noting that *"Der Begriff der Nachfolge ist das Stiefkind der evangelischen Ethik."*[70]

That *Discipleship* is a work of ethics is not denied. Bonhoeffer's ethical methodology is apparent from the first paragraph of the work, giving an important clue to its interpretation, one which frames the entirety of the work's contents.[71] The echo of his ever-probing question, "Who is Jesus Christ for us today?" is rendered here in two questions: "What did Jesus want to say to us?" and "What does he want from us today?" Although *Discipleship* has become a timeless work, boosted in large part by its broad appeal beyond the academy, it is truly applied theology in a crucial historical moment.[72] If one loses the autobiographical nature and historically pressing occasion of the document, if one loses the questions superintending the entire scope of the book and the hurriedness of the age that desperately required a theological response, one loses Bonhoeffer's ethical methodology in the process. It is to this we now turn.

Of the most important sections in this work that address the question of peace, the following excerpt is well known:

> Jesus' followers are called to peace. When Jesus called them, they found their peace. Jesus is their peace. Now they are not only to have peace, but they are to make peace. To do this they *renounce violence and strife*. Those things never help the cause of Christ. Christ's kingdom is a realm of peace, and those in Christ's community greet each other with a greeting of peace. Jesus' disciples maintain peace by choosing to suffer instead of causing others to suffer. They preserve community when others destroy it. They renounce self-assertion and are silent in the face of hatred

---

70. "The concept of discipleship is the poor cousin of Protestant ethics" (my translation). (Runestam, "Die Nachfolge Jesu," 747).

71. *DBWE* 6, 5.

72. For example, the discussion surrounding cheap grace has as much to do with a general danger of abusing one's walk in Christ as it has to do with the Confessing Church's inability to react determinately against the Reich Church and National Socialism.

and injustice. That is how they overcome evil with good. That is how they are makers of divine peace in a world of hatred and war. But their peace will never be greater than when they encounter evil people in peace and are willing to suffer from them. Peacemakers will bear the cross with their Lord, for peace was made at the cross.[73]

Bonhoeffer seems clear that violence has no place in the gospel message of Christ. The question remains whether the renunciation of violence should be understood as a thoroughgoing advocacy of pacifism. One might ask, for example, do those who keep silent before hatred and injustice do so because they renounce violence *in principiis* or because they are reoriented into the ethic of Christ? It is notable that in the very next section of *DBW*, both the German and English editors point to a footnote on Bethge's own notes from the *Nachlass Dietrich Bonhoeffer* where he asserts that "everything is renunciation."[74] The reason given by Bethge refuses any distinction between active and passive ethical decision making. Bonhoeffer's use of the term *Verzicht auf* for renunciation is notable here for two reasons. Besides appearing in the two examples above, this term is appropriated once more in Bonhoeffer's comments on the beatitude, "Blessed are the pure of heart, for they will see God." Here the German reads:

> *Das reine Herz ist das einfältige Herz des Kindes, das nicht weiß um Gut and Böse, das Herz Adams vor dem Fall, das Herz, in dem nicht das Gewissen, sondern Jesu Wille herrscht. Wer im Verzicht steht auf das eigene Gute und Böse, auf das eigene Herz, wer so in der Buße steht, und allein an Jesus hängt, dessen Herz ist rein durch das Wort Jesu.*[75]

---

73. *DBWE* 4, 108.

74. Ibid., 4, 109, n. 43.

75. "The pure heart is the simple heart of a child, who does not know about good and evil, the heart of Adam before the Fall, the heart, in which the will of Jesus rules, rather than the conscience. Who in renunciation of one's own good and evil stands, of one's own heart, who thus stands in repentance, and depends on Jesus alone, whose heart is pure through Jesus' word" (my translation). (Bonhoeffer, *Nachfolge* (Werke 4), 107).

Should the renunciation of violence and strife expressed in the aforementioned passage (*Verzicht auf Gewalt und Aufruhr*) be rendered as a deontological ethical response by the doer of God's word or as a response in the context of Bonhoeffer's ethics of relationship where context not commandment is crucial?[76] In keeping with previous interpretative clues, renunciation does not appear to be a decision that must be made, as it were, from the imposition of an ethical dilemma. Instead, renunciation is grafted into one's orientation, extending beyond the limitations of good and evil as an act of discipleship in Christ. In this way, Bonhoeffer's relational ethics seems appropriately inferred. Another interesting matter is that in all three passages mentioned above that pertain to *Verzicht auf*, the English translation renders a verb where, by contrast, the German renders a noun in combination with a preposition. It seems reasonable to infer that the part of speech the word takes in German is critical to its own theological meaning, so that in changing that part of speech for purposes of a smoother translation into English may actually create a loss of meaning. Renunciation conceived as a existential response to a theological imperative comes in the act of losing oneself to the world to find one's life in Christ. Such action creates a new ontological relationship that cannot be exhausted by the many forms an act of renunciation might take. In contrast, where renunciation might be conceived as an action originating in its verbal form, the act of renouncing is limited by any number of specific scenarios that run the risk of absolutizing concrete action. Renunciation alone begs the question of what kind of renouncing I am doing, an answer that only the person involved can give rather than broad appeals to a *renunciation de jure*, making any authoritative manifestation outside of Christ deliberately vague, but entirely personal (as I am the one answering the command), while ensuring that the term cannot be confined to any one commandment. Bethge's notion that "everything is renunciation" supports such an interpretation.

---

76. Both passages where the term *Verzicht auf* appears are italicized in the German for special attention.

Another question relating to the issue of peace in Bonhoeffer's *Discipleship* is the use of *eirēnopoioi* in Matthew 5:9, which can be translated as "those who make peace." The use of this passage perhaps should not be confused with a formal distinction deriving from a doctrine of pure pacifism.[77]

Finally, Bonhoeffer asserts that the peacemakers are those who suffer.[78] Although suffering and *theologia crucis* are topics with an important history of interpretation in Bonhoeffer scholarship, it is enough to say that Bonhoeffer believes suffering is a path to peacemaking, for he calls to mind the peace won for humanity at the cross.[79] The application of suffering like renunciation in *Discipleship* is experienced concretely but is also born in relationship to Christ. If we leave suffering as an abstract concept that is only left to Christ on the cross, then we lose the concrete nature of that suffering. One might suffer the physical indignation of his enemy, and like Bonhoeffer, one might suffer psychological damage in facing the state-sponsored radicalism of Nazi Germany by fighting doubts, fears, and temptations to flee its frenzy. Let us not forget that Bonhoeffer struggled with this temptation, having traveled to London in 1933 and then to New York again in 1939. Bonhoeffer was well aware that the consequence of concrete peacemaking under the Nazi regime was censorship, isolation, imprisonment, and even death. He was already experiencing the consequences of censorship by 1936.[80] Bonhoeffer's activities went against the grain

---

77. The editors of *DBWE* draw attention to the double meaning of *eirēnopoioi* and note in Luther's commentary it has a more robust meaning than simply passivity. Quoting *WA Deutsche Bibel* 6:26, the commentary on Matthew 5:9 reads "those who make, further, and preserve peace among people, as Christ has made peace for us with God . . . they are more than the peaceable" (*DBWE* 4, 108).

78. Ibid., 108.

79. *DBWE* 15, 3/2, 473–75.

80. On March 7, 1936, Theodor Heckel wrote to the Regional Church Committee insinuating Bonhoeffer should be considered a pacifist and enemy of the state (*Staatsfeind*) and should no longer train theologians (see *DBWE* 14, 1B/58, 148). Bethge regarded the introduction of the Nuremberg Laws from 1935 the decisive factor in Bonhoeffer's arrest in 1943 (see Boehlke and Drake, *Dietrich Bonhoeffer: Memories and Perspective*s).

of national sentiment, were unpopular, and at worst, moved him and his listeners toward treason. This concern resonates in his later writing where he expresses fears that his legacy will be sacrificed to misunderstanding and contempt.

There is still one more passage in *Discipleship* that Tödt considers the most important; it is on peace. It occurs as commentary on Matthew 5:43-48 under the title "The Enemy—'The Extraordinary.'"[81] Bonhoeffer locates the core ethic in this biblical passage, which he finds beyond the ethical boundary of good and evil, in the presence of Christ. The overcoming of good and evil here is reminiscent of his early theology in Barcelona, though this relationship is not often emphasized. Just as he preached in his lecture "Basic Questions of a Christian Ethic" in Barcelona, the enemy must be encountered with love.[82] Although Bonhoeffer makes no attempt to appeal to casuistry to punctuate ethical dilemmas, the concrete advice he gives is a close approximation. Alluding to Psalm 109:4, he asserts that one must pray for his enemies.[83] He adds to this a prediction of the future in which he sees a unity of congregations lifting holy hands in prayer, demonstrating their allegiance to Christ and their love for their enemy.

While some single references occur to doing good works for one's enemy, it is noteworthy that peace is not mentioned in these latter passages of *Discipleship*. Rather, Bonhoeffer places new emphasis on the one-directional nature of Christian love for enemies who *remain* enemies and are not won over to Christ. Furthermore, one could justifiably argue, that peace is not at all the concern, for Bonhoeffer states, "*Nicht nur duldend sollen wir das Böse und den Bösen ertragen, nicht nur Schlag nicht mit Widerschlag vergelten, sondern in herzlicher Liebe sollen wir unserem Feinde zugetan sein.*"[84] Instead of peace, Bonhoeffer is calling for the rejection of

81. Tödt, *Authentic Faith*, 140; see also *DBWE* 4, 137-45.
82. *DBWE* 10, 370-371.
83. "Because I love them, they are against me; but I pray" (my translation). "*Dafür, daß ich sie liebe, sind sie wider mich; ich aber bete*" (Psalm 109:4, Luther Bibel).
84. "Not only should we endure [*duldend*] to bear evil and the evil one, not

a *doctrine of retribution*, which itself does not bar all violence but determines only limitations on its expression.

Emphasis on suffering in *Discipleship* represents a new dimension in Bonhoeffer's thinking. Is this suffering a natural outcome of absorbing an enemy's hatred and violence? Or is this suffering a pietistic response in which one suffers because he refuses to act out *in principiis* where the command might be interpreted as a commitment to nonviolence? One may answer with an eye to Bonhoeffer's *theologia crucis*. At the cross, Jesus did not experience spiritual suffering on account of not avenging himself but truly suffered in the flesh. Bonhoeffer's view of suffering here has less to do with pacifism and more to do with the consequences of resisting. In one such example, he suggests those who "preserve community when others destroy it" experience the trauma of suffering.[85] Preservation, however, is not a reaction that occurs *when* others destroy community but rather is an orientation in contrast to those forces *where* community is destroyed. This last insight offers a rather tantalizing image of Bonhoeffer's future activities. While he actively looked for solutions to bring about peace, preserving the Christian witness against the ideological community of Nazism would prove an act of suffering that in no way necessitated an appeal to pacifism, yet could be integrated into the contextualism of his theological method.

It is my conclusion that the shape of the most important passages on peace in *Discipleship* continues to point to the primary importance of a relationship with Christ, and that these passages argue for contextual priority rather than an approach that warrants absolute pacifism. Passages found in *Discipleship*, such as the examples mentioned above, continue to root out the question

---

only refuse to repay a blow with a blow, but in sincere love we should be fond of our enemies." Note: DBWE 6, 139, ignores *duldend* (present participle of *dulden*) and translates the sentence instead as "bear . . . passively," probably to avoid an awkward construction, but as a result this translation creates a meaning that I would argue is not suggested (Bonhoeffer, *Nachfolge*, 142).

85. Bonhoeffer, *Nachfolge*, 108; the German rendering is a bit different: "*sie bewahren Gemeinschaft, wo der Andere sie bricht . . .*" The concept of "the Other" (singular) is important in Bonhoeffer's theology (see chapter 2).

of right and wrong as a standard of ethical judgment. Instead, peace is prioritized as an orientation found in Christ. As context remains critical to the way in which Bonhoeffer thought about the theological task, emphasis on peace makes sense at the time in which *Discipleship* was written, and as a nonviolent, peaceable solution remained a viable option in the international ecumenical church. Peace was the command that Christ was speaking to his church. What *Discipleship* does do well, however, is to challenge the appropriateness of peace as a question that can even be asked seriously before it first must be confronted within the theological framework of one's relationship to Christ. It is in that relationship alone where peace must take its form.

A Call to Arms: Bonhoeffer and Military Service

One way in which Bonhoeffer has been labeled a pacifist is by statements in his writing that directly challenge the call to active duty. With the dangerous situation in Germany not entirely manifest, Bonhoeffer could bluntly assert that "serving in the military defies God."[86] He could warn his international audience of fellow believers that Christians ought not to take up arms against one another since to do so was to take up arms against Christ himself.[87] Bonhoeffer had indeed filed for conscientious objector status, but was denied, and even pressed the point to his fiancée, Maria von Wedemeyer, while in jail. He also knew upon returning to Germany in September 1939 that he would be confronted with enlistment once again, since nearly 98 percent of seminarians and many Protestant clergy were being called to active duty. Bonhoeffer and Bethge desperately attempted to avoid military service at the beginning of the war.[88] Bonhoeffer resolved to apply as an Army chaplain in an attempt to avoid service on the front, but this too was denied.[89] Yet

---

86. *DBWE* 12, 2/6, 260.
87. Kelly and Nelson, *Testament to Freedom*, 228.
88. *DBWE* 16, 5.
89. Bethge, *Dietrich Bonhoeffer: A Biography*, 666.

it was the work he was doing in the resistance movement, and not an absolute stance against war, that was propelling these actions.

Despite deep disappointments and frustrations within the church, Bonhoeffer demonstrated a nonjudgmental tact toward fellow Christians who were struggling to find their own response to Nazi Socialism. A handful of examples demonstrate this.

At his seminary in Finkenwalde (1935–1937), while his students were being called to active duty, Bonhoeffer did not protest their departure or threaten to cut them off from fellowship. Renate Wind makes this point:

> Not all members of the Finkenwalde course sustained radical opposition. Regularly, one of them would go to the "consistory" and have himself legalized and appointed by the church committees. The social and family pressure was too great, above all of those with less generous support. Dietrich would not approve of them, but he would understand. He was well aware of his privileges: with his social connections and his family background he would always get by.[90]

This attitude is noteworthy in a handful of cases: In a circular letter from May 1940 to former Finkenwalde brothers serving on the front, Bonhoeffer sympathizes with the questions they are asking. But Bonhoeffer never advises in a way that would demoralize them or require a particular stand for pacifism be set forward. In those cases, Bonhoeffer recognizes the impossibility of ministry, writing to those who find it difficult to remain a Christian that "one cannot as a soldier simply go on leading the life of a pastor, and one should not torment oneself internally about this."[91] It is

---

90. Wind, *Dietrich Bonhoeffer: A Spoke in the Wheel*, 107.

91. Brocker points to the language in *DBWE* 16, 1/151, 264–65) from one of the Finkenwalde Circular Letters, asserting that Bonhoeffer bitterly opposed the legalization of pastors by way of the 1937 Himmler decree because the same could force candidates into situations where the gospel is compromised. But this point seems exaggerated to me. The opinion that every man does what is right according to his conscience and before God is consistent with Bonhoeffer's advice during this time. Bonhoeffer even goes so far as to stir up reflection, in particular that one cannot unrestrictedly accept the assertions

worth noting that his influence on his Berlin confirmation class in 1931 produced friendships that endured, and among this cohort were avowed Nazis.[92] De Gruchy notes that even when speaking to his students, Bonhoeffer encouraged them to be conscientious objectors, even though he did not demand of them nonviolent resistance, only that they "take Jesus' teaching about peace making seriously."[93] In another circular letter, most likely from March 1, 1942, Bonhoeffer memorializes the lives of three of his former students killed in the line of duty. Again, there is no attempt at absolution, and no condemnation. The difficulties of the day are acknowledged in this letter, and beyond one's own moral reservations, Bonhoeffer reminds readers that there is hope in the Scriptures to overcome such struggles.[94]

Hans von Wedemeyer was killed on August 22, 1942, on the Eastern Front. In a letter to Frau von Wedemeyer, Bonhoeffer, who was interested in her daughter Maria, recalls that Maria's father was a noble Christian, one who raised his family in the church. Bethge suggests that the elder von Wedemeyer suffered from inner conflict about the war, but there is no such reflection in Bonhoeffer's letter to Frau von Wedemeyer. Likewise, Bonhoeffer never imposes his ethical convictions in the letter.[95] According to Bonhoeffer, Maria's father was in heaven. If Bonhoeffer was only hoping to play for the affections of Maria at the expense of a few disingenuous words to her mother, it would be unusual given the person he presented to us in so many of his letters. This is demonstrated in his concern against taking advantage of the woman when the elder von Wedemeyer asks that Bonhoeffer and Maria make space from one another.

A final depiction that challenges a Bonhoeffer who at this time was resolutely committed to pacifism comes from Joachim

---

made at Dahlem that no cooperation ought to be given to the Reich Church without taking personal responsibility for his own decisions.

92. Robertson, *The Shame and the Sacrifice*, 74.
93. De Gruchy, *Confessions of a Christian Humanist*, 146–47.
94. *DBWE* 16, 1/144, 253–55.
95. Bethge, *Dietrich Bonhoeffer: A Biography*, 693–94.

Kanitz, one of Bonhoeffer's students who sat under his instruction in Finkenwalde.[96] In an interview, Kanitz explains how he went to see Bonhoeffer after having been assigned to fight on the Russian front. As he stood before Bonhoeffer in full military regalia, he felt ashamed because he knew the kind of work Bonhoeffer was most likely doing in the resistance. To his surprise, Bonhoeffer pointed to a medal on Kanitz's uniform and asked him what it was for. Kanitz recalls how there was no condemnation or judgment. Kanitz himself decided in this moment to swear off war because of the kind and unexpected nature of his professor's response.[97]

The question of whether the increasing personal pressure to enlist contributed to Bonhoeffer's sympathetic responses to others is an important question. But the question itself does not appear to be the right one, for it assumes that Bonhoeffer was committed to a specific expression of pacifism. When one considers the liberty permitted in his own theology, such interactions with others can help us to understand Bonhoeffer's responses more sensibly instead of the rigid pacifist who is caught in the miasma of ideological stasis. If abstract principles could not be the substance of one's relationship with God, how could Bonhoeffer require of others not to follow their own conscience or demand their experience conform to his? One sees this in Bonhoeffer's early writing about his concept of community:

> God does not desire a history of individual human beings, but the history of the human community. However, God does not want a community that absorbs the individual into itself, but a community of human beings. In God's eyes, community and individual exist in the same moment and rest in one another. The collective unit and the individual unit have the same structure in God's eyes. On these basic-relations rest the concepts of the religious community and the church.[98]

---

96. Ibid., 425.
97. Boehlke and Drake, *Dietrich Bonhoeffer: Memories and Perspectives*.
98. *DBWE* 1, 80.

The fundamental connection between the individual who must be allowed to maintain his individuality yet who cannot exist outside the community is a theme in Bonhoeffer with persistent application.

Does Bonhoeffer Reject War?

In the 1959 foreword to *The Cost of Discipleship*, Gerhard Leibholz, Bonhoeffer's brother-in-law, states that what Bonhoeffer rejected was a war of aggression.[99] Rasmussen argues that Bonhoeffer was a "provisional pacifist" for whom any kind of war had to be judged by its individual merits.[100] When Bonhoeffer says "today, there must be no more war—the cross will not have it," like many of his statements, it is always with qualification.[101] During this same period, Bonhoeffer warns that the church cannot simply say "do not engage in war." If such a statement but the recipient to whom the command is directed is left unresolved, says Bonhoeffer, then the responsibility of interpretation as well is unresolved. But because any command to the Christian is likewise an address the community of saints, the church must be prepared to speak clearly and definitely. The community cannot be divided. The command itself must be unifying. Perhaps the most expedient way to read Bonhoeffer's approach is not as a mechanistic desire for unanimity that suggests a political process, but as one that takes seriously the relationships between individuals cultivated in a community that makes its mission obedience to Christ. Such a reading seems faithful to Bonhoeffer's sociological emphasis on the church as a collective person whose task is proclamation. The church's capacity to receive the command should be no different than the individual's ability. Moreover, the commandment comes with absolute authority within the context of each interpretative moment. Bonhoeffer writes, "The word of the church here and now must be a valid,

---

99. Bonhoeffer, *Cost of Discipleship*, 17.

100. Rasmussen notes that Bonhoeffer does not rule out wars of aggression (*Dietrich Bonhoeffer: Reality and Resistance*, 99).

101. Kelly and Nelson, *Testament to Freedom*, 104.

binding word. Someone can only speak to me with authority if a word from the deepest knowledge of my humanity encounters me here and now in all my reality."[102]

A relevant entry for the catechism he was developing in 1936 raises the difficulty of the subject matter. Here he strikes through several questions: "May a Christian take part in war?" And then again, "What does God say to war?" He finally settles on the following:

> How should the Christian conduct himself in war? . . . Here there is no clear command of God. The Church can never bless war and weapons. The Christian can never take part in an unjust war. If the Christian takes up the sword he will call to God daily for forgiveness of the sin and for peace.[103]

Various responses have emerged in reference to this period. Bethge blames Bonhoeffer's indecision to condemn war on the issue of convincing the catechetical candidates of his own personal rejection of war.[104] Rasmussen chooses to focus on the language of "just war" as an escape from absolute pacifism.[105]

Yet beyond these explanations that have the effect of exonerating Bonhoeffer on the basis of the details, one should consider the interpretative possibility, consistent with my position, that the command given by God is a command one must approach in simple obedience and in the full confidence of faith. Only when this is achieved, can one treat each command with irrevocable force for the individual because in living in the openness required of a relationship, responding is the condition that authenticates the eternity of the command, rather than the proclamation itself that fails to grasp the individual in his freedom to respond.

---

102. Ibid., 98.
103. Schlingensiepen, *Dietrich Bonhoeffer, 1906–1945*, 109.
104. Bethge, *Dietrich Bonhoeffer: A Biography*, 188.
105. Rasmussen, *Dietrich Bonhoeffer: Reality and Resistance*, 107.

Bonhoeffer and the Quest for Peace

Love at the Center of Relational Ethics

Peace has an undeniable resonance in Bonhoeffer's ethical methodology because peace represents the constitutive character of the gospel. At the same time, scholars like Rasmussen warn that Bonhoeffer himself "says little of a directly definitive nature" about peace.[106] At times, Bonhoeffer's generic statements demonstrate Rasmussen's observation: "Jesus calls his followers to peace, and Jesus himself is that peace."[107] But statements such as this should not mean that Bonhoeffer does not appropriate peace in a way that is inscrutable to analysis.

For Bonhoeffer, one is oriented to Christ according to divine peace, but that peace takes no abstract form whereby universal acceptance is assumed outside its concrete form. Yet despite this emphasis on the concrete in his Christological ethics, the historical mode of peace is multifarious and confusing, for here too the commandment to peace may not *look* like peace; it may take on the appearance of violence, it may be a militant peace of struggle (*Kampf*),[108] or it may even require just wars. How then does Bonhoeffer prioritize peace in his ethical method?

The distinction between love as the highest commandment and center of Bonhoeffer's Christological ethics and divine expressions of peace, mercy, and forgiveness, or any number of other attributes, is often difficult to tease apart because the latter expressions are inextricably implied in Christian love. God is love. Christ is the reality of that love. But Bonhoeffer also is clear that Christ is our peace. Christ makes peace for us at the cross. Nevertheless, these attributive expressions in themselves are unhelpful unless contextualized. Bonhoeffer's own disdain for abstraction as *Prinzip* recalls a certain ontological understanding that he inherits from Seeberg on the being of God—where faith is, God is also, and where faith is not, God is not.[109] Bonhoeffer later develops this concept in that

---

106. Ibid., 95.
107. *DBWE* 4, 108.
108. Rasmussen, *Dietrich Bonhoeffer: Reality and Resistance*, 102.
109. Floyd, "Encounter with an Other," 117.

God's reality is made known to us only because the world's reality rests in Christ—whether we know it or not. However, where we *do* know it, we apprehend it in faith. Bonhoeffer appears to leave open the possibility that God's sustaining the world, which originates in Christ's formation in the reality of the world, means that one can also experience and even respond in love and peace without knowledge of Christ. This possibility remains because God appeals to us not as an idealistic but ethical reality. Bonhoeffer does however stop short of suggesting equivalence between those who appropriate the reality of God through faith against those who appropriate the reality of God without faith.[110] Love forms the basis of our relationship, primarily because it is God who condescends to us in love. This love comes to us while we are enemies. As Green paraphrases Bonhoeffer: "We are all enemies of God: The enemies of God are not just those we consider our enemies; above all it is we ourselves who are the enemies of God."[111] What comes of this, however, is a concept of equivalence that merges peace and love into an indistinguishable parity. As Green writes, "For Bonhoeffer, the Christian peace ethic is at the centre of the gospel," while in the very same paragraph, Green asserts, "love of enemies belongs to the heart and substance of the gospel."[112] At this point, if we are pressed to say anything about love and peace other than that they occupy precisely the same conceptual ground, we are left with meaningfully little. On the surface, Bonhoeffer does little to work out these concepts satisfactorily. Because of this, it could be argued that we gain nothing in our knowledge of peace and love as separate concepts or even similar ones, for the distinctions appear useless, except to aggregate our existing theological layers of expression.

How might our perception of Bonhoeffer be rescued in a way that helps distinguish between these two concepts? Although it appears that in Bonhoeffer's conceptual framework, peace cannot be imagined as anything other than God's love, I would argue that the

110. *DBWE* 6, 334.
111. Green, "Pacifism and Tyrannicide," 38.
112. Ibid.

same cannot be said for love. One of the most striking examples of this is found in both early and late stages in Bonhoeffer's writing in which he asserts that God's love is expressed in judgment and wrath.[113] A state of judgment is hardly consistent with a state of peace. It is not enough to say that where God commands peace, peace is there, so long as one remains committed to concrete reality.

Furthermore, it appears at times that Bonhoeffer relegates the importance of peace to a lesser position. "It is not pacifism that is the victory which overcomes the world (1 John 5:4), but faith, which expects everything from God and hopes in the coming of Christ and his Kingdom."[114] Here we must be careful given the distinction made between peace and pacifism. The idea that faith, and not peace, is our victory raises the question of how foundational and methodologically proper is peace to our relational experience of Christ if we understand that in relating to Christ we are always relating to others as well, and in particular, enemies who may remain our enemies.

Bonhoeffer asserts that we are to love our enemies despite any possibility of receiving love in return. Our actions are never predicated on a particular response. In *Discipleship* he even states that those who do to us evil are worthy of even greater love![115] It is informative to note here what Green sees as the traditional movement of God toward humanity in Bonhoeffer's theology: "Love of enemies is not just a single discrete command of Jesus in the Sermon on the Mount. Love of enemies belongs to the heart and substance of the gospel. Without God's love of enemies there is no

113. For example, during his Barcelona days, Bonhoeffer comments that wrath and love bear themselves in God's essence as contradictory elements, to which his Union professor Eugene William Lyman answers, "Are these contradictory?" (*DBWE* 10, 2/16, 455); "In Christ, God's wrath is revealed as nowhere else, yet at the same time God's grace is revealed as nowhere else." Kelly and Nelson, *Testament to Freedom*, 181; And the again "The incarnation of God (i.e., the incarnation of love) would be misunderstood if one did not also want to understand the worldly orders of the strict justice, punishment, and wrath of God as the fulfillment of this incarnate love . . ." (*DBWE* 16, 2/13, 548-49).

114. *DBWE* 13, 2/2, 306.

115. *DBWE* 4, 141.

reconciliation, no grace, no forgiveness, no salvation."[116] To this we may add there is also no peace.

For Bonhoeffer then, love is the highest commandment and activity of God because it is tied to God's revelation of himself in Jesus. Bonhoeffer's analysis of the importance of love in 1 Corinthians 13 is instructive with regard to the priority of love. One might have all powers of prophecy, understand all mysteries, walk in a powerful faith, and even maintain a disposition to love, and yet not have love. What is this love?

> God is love, that is, love is not a human behavior, sentiment, or deed, but it is God who is love. What love is can be known only by one who knows God; the reverse is not true, that one would first know what love is—that is, from nature—and therefore also know what God is . . . Love is God's self-revelation.[117]

Yet, as Timothy P. Jackson rightly notes, "The *imitatio Christi* provides the concrete meaning of charity. One is not left with a pure *via negativa* leading to an inscrutable transcendental virtue."[118] Bonhoeffer himself asserts that:

> Love is always God himself. Love is always God's revelation in Jesus Christ. However, the strictest concentration of all thoughts and statements about love on the name of Jesus Christ now must not reduce this name to an abstract concept. Instead, this name must always be understood in the concrete richness of the historical reality of a living human being.[119]

The name of Jesus must not suffer a holy consecration that robs us of an authentic openness to the changing demands of the concrete world. Again, Bonhoeffer discharges the aggrandizing terms of idealism in favor of the world of relational living. The propositional-rationalistic apologetic that attempts an explanation

---

116. Green, "Pacifism and Tyrannicide," 38.
117. *DBWE* 6, 334.
118. Jackson, "Church, World, and Christian Charity," 97.
119. *DBWE* 6, 335.

for the nature of God's being cannot effectively deconstruct a phenomenology of immanent opportunities where robust theological participation remains.

The attributes of God and the name of Jesus are bound to this concrete reality and its ever-changing expression.[120] *Relationship* remains Bonhoeffer's interpretative filter and requires that the attributes of God are not simply semantic signs whose real meaning points us to the undifferentiated oneness of God, but rather that these attributes are meaningfully applied as God is revealed, that is, the operation of God's attributes illumines the relationship between God and humanity. In positing a merciful, loving, jealous, or wrathful God, Bonhoeffer's intention is not to understand these attributes based upon an epistemological assent to a general prin-

---

120. This insight is particularly important with regard to the rejection of the scholastic doctrine of divine simplicity as seen, for example, in Bonhoeffer's contemporary Brunner (cf. chapter 1, n. 89). Although Aquinas is associated with a philosophical defense of the doctrine, his understanding of how the names of God functioned within the human sphere of activity is worth noting. Aquinas asserts the following: "Some relative names are imposed to signify the relative habitudes themselves, as 'master' and 'servant,' 'father,' and 'son,' and the like, and these relatives are called predicamental [*secundum esse*]. But others are imposed to signify the things from which ensue certain habitudes, as the mover and the thing moved, the head and the thing that has a head, and the like: and these relatives are called transcendental [*secundum dici*]. Thus, there is the same two-fold difference in divine names. For some signify the habitude itself to the creature, as 'Lord,' and these do not signify the divine substance directly, but indirectly, in so far as they presuppose the divine substance; as dominion presupposes power, which is the divine substance. Others signify the divine essence directly, and consequently the corresponding habitudes, as 'Savior,' 'Creator,' and suchlike; and these signify the action of God, which is His essence. Yet both names are said of God temporarily so far as they imply a habitude either principally or consequently, but not as signifying the essence, either directly or indirectly." (*ST* 1, Q. 13, Art. 7.)

Aquinas agreed there was a reality to the way humans relate to God, but he considered these phenomena of a relative order. While Bonhoeffer agrees we are dealing with relative language, like many of his contemporaries, his writings trend in a direction that rejects relativity as a subordinate means of revelation and rejects attempts to recover an epistemology of the nature of God as a dangerous and impossible effort. Unlike Aquinas's position, a mode of knowing *in principle* would bear little difference from a mode of knowing based in God's essence, and both are rejected.

ciple of knowing, but to illuminate God's presence in the person of Christ. To speak otherwise would be to render the language of theological participation into one of submission.

Conclusion

What I have hoped to demonstrate in this chapter is that Bonhoeffer's move to a more intense support of peace should not be mistaken for ideological pacifism, nor should his intellectual development be regarded as a move towards an eventually concession to violence. Rather Bonhoeffer's "pacifism" appears both in his early and later writings and is not easily compartmentalized *because* it was bound to a dynamic notion of ethical relationship through which its very expression was subject to change, according to the permissions granted within his own methodology. Likewise, Bonhoeffer's pacifism is situationally diffuse, located at one and the same time in both the sacred and the secular—as both our orientation to God and as a commandment by God. The question of whether Bonhoeffer was then an absolute or provisional pacifist is the wrong question with regard to his theology, precisely because absolute pacifism is confronted by the *historic moment* and provisional pacifism is confronted by our *orientation in Christ*. In Bonhoeffer's ethics, one cannot be an absolute or provisional pacifist with respect to Christ.

---- 4 ----

Bonhoeffer and the Question of Murder

*"Es ist uns besser ein Mensch sterbe für das Volk,
denn daß das ganze Volk verderbe."*

—JOHANNES 11.50[1]

IN THE PREVIOUS CHAPTER we looked at Bonhoeffer's relationship to the question of peace. The concept of peace and the ideology of pacifism required analysis before the question could be raised about how Bonhoeffer approached the activity of peacemaking. This investigation revealed that the path to practical peacemaking solutions is not simple, particularly because Bonhoeffer's interest in peace hinges on a theological rather than political interpretation. Furthermore, his rejection of peace that originates in the world in opposition to peace that comes from God makes a phenomenologically constrained identification of the concept impossible, because peace outside of Christ is verisimilitude at best. Bonhoeffer's reflection on the Sermon on the Mount examines this situation. Bonhoeffer reminds us that Jesus blesses the peacemakers in their desire for peace but provides nothing specific about how that peace should operate.

We are now in a position to examine the important relationship between peace and murder. Like the concept of peace, Haynes

1. Luther 1912 translation.

reminds us that Bonhoeffer's attitude toward violence is complex.[2] An important question will linger throughout this examination: If Bonhoeffer became convinced that the path to peace could only be realized through the murder of Hitler, does he undermine his own integrity as a peacemaker? Of course, this question assumes that certain ethical parameters are already settled that would consequently indict Bonhoeffer of moral wrongdoing. I will again analyze and bring into the conversation Bonhoeffer's methodological approach.

Bonhoeffer on War, While in Barcelona

During Bonhoeffer's Barcelona days, the reality of National Socialism had not become a pressing problem that required an urgent response. So while Bonhoeffer's comments may not serve as direct confrontations with an evil not yet known, he had known the guilt of Versailles, the aftermath of war, and was still prepared to speak about the paradox of God's commandments with these considerations as his background. Bonhoeffer made his first serious move into ethics during a series of sermons and lectures he delivered as an assistant pastor to a German congregation in Barcelona. He was eager to fill his time meaningfully amid his own complaints of idle time and monotonous work.[3]

In his last of three lectures he gave during 1929, Bonhoeffer looks at the nature of Christian ethics. The context of this lecture is important because it takes up the question of murder by way of a poignant and problematic example. Bonhoeffer begins the lecture by questioning normative ethical thinking.

> In speaking today about basic questions of a Christian ethic, we do not intend to embark on the essentially hopeless attempt to present universally valid Christian

2. Haynes, *Bonhoeffer Phenomenon*, 94.

3. Robertson writes that there was no intellectual stimulus from the congregation, and he most likely tried to raise the bar himself by offering stimulating topics to a people who otherwise led moral lives (*The Shame and the Sacrifice*, 46–47).

Bonhoeffer and the Question of Murder

norms and commandments applicable to contemporary ethical questions. We intend instead merely to examine and to participate in the peculiar movement of ethical problems in today's world from the perspective of basic Christian ideas. The deepest reason why we confine ourselves in this manner is that, as we will see in greater depth later, there are no and cannot be Christian norms and principles of a moral nature. Only in the actual execution of a given action do the concepts of "good" and "bad" apply, that is, only in the given present moment: hence any attempt to explicate principles is like trying to draw a bird in flight.[4]

Bonhoeffer continues by raising the question of whether the Sermon on the Mount really has anything unique to say to us given that the ancient world also had its share of thinkers who set forth moral guidelines that were similar to those posited by Christ. Bonhoeffer then moves to examine what he presents as a German Christian position on war. He writes that a Christian ought not to kill, and he invokes the Sermon on the Mount. Nevertheless, he points out that Christian men still go to war, the same men who "hold services of worship in the field and dare drag God and the holy name of Jesus Christ into the horrific murder . . ."[5] On the surface, Bonhoeffer has pointed out what appears to be a compelling contradiction of moral common sense. Furthermore, the strong language seems to favor the stronger emphasis on peace that Bonhoeffer adopted in the 1930s. Yet he follows with ethical reasoning that is demonstrative of his ethical method: "This seems entirely clear and convincing, yet it suffers at the central issue: it is not concrete and as a result does not look into the depths of the Christian decision. It invokes the commandment not to kill and believes that commandment to be the solution."[6]

Bonhoeffer proceeds with a relevant ethical dilemma. Here, a man must decide whether to stop an enemy soldier by killing him to save his family, or otherwise that man must stand by helplessly

4. *DBWE* 10, 2/3, 359–60.
5. Ibid., 2/3, 370.
6. Ibid.

and allow the soldier to kill his mother and brother in order to fulfill his obligation to the commandment. Perhaps what is most interesting in Bonhoeffer's analysis is that in this passage he focuses not on the prohibitive nature of murder but on the choice of *who* to murder as a way to draw out the insufficiency of the commandment.

As a principle of conduct, the commandment not to murder fails because by sparing his enemy, the individual becomes responsible for the murder of his kin at the hands of the enemy. Bonhoeffer uses this example effectively to exploit the tension between the moral law and the loyalty a good German feels toward family and nation.[7] The answer Bonhoeffer gives remains a subject of controversy in Bonhoeffer scholarship: "God gave me my mother, my people. For what I have, I thank my people; what I am, I am through my people, and so what I have should also belong to my people; that is in the divine order [*Ordnung*] of things, for God created the peoples."[8]

The impulse to defend one's family seems so natural that Tödt admits "it is not easy to detect the fine rift cracking argument here."[9] He goes on to assert that Bonhoeffer abandons the moment for a "para-situational order." Green has likewise criticized Bonhoeffer on this point for recommending a course of action that embraces his own people before other people. And so Green writes that Bonhoeffer "takes refuge in two embarrassing claims: (1) that God established in creation a divine order of peoples (*Völker*) so that one's first loyalty is to one's own people,[10] and (2) that Chris-

---

7. Situating this example in ultra-nationalistic ideology, especially given that the enemy seems to imply the foreigner, ignores Bonhoeffer's deep and affectionate engagement of foreigners (the Italians, the Spanish) and cultural curiosity, and is de-emphasized in Bonhoefferian scholarship.

8. *DBWE* 10, 2/3, 371.

9. Tödt, *Authentic Faith*, 117.

10. Yet the concept of people (*Volk*) was not simply qualified by a divine order of people if by this one means race. Reich theologians like Althaus could express the significant nature of race while at the same time admitting it was not altogether binding: "Among the factors which determine and make up a *Volk*, the community of blood and race have become decisively important for

tians pray for their enemies even while killing them and being killed by them."[11] Like Tödt, Green also comments that Bonhoeffer strikes a contradiction between the call to do ethics in the moment and the inherent responsibility to one's people (*Volk*).[12] Despite Rasmussen's more sympathetic reading of Bonhoeffer as being a provisional pacifist who still allows for just wars, Rasmussen notes the shift from Barcelona in the catechism put together by Bonhoeffer and Franz Hildebrandt in which they condemn "a national boast based on flesh and blood" as "a sin against the Spirit."[13] Most scholars have concluded that this early sermon, for one reason or another, is something of a misstep that cannot comfortably be fitted within Bonhoeffer's latter work.[14]

Yet despite this, Tödt warns that while the use of some language was current in national Protestantism at the time, it nonetheless serves a particular function in the lecture and must not be "torn" out of its context. He notes that "Bonhoeffer's conception of 1929 was certainly not 'pre-fascistic,'" concluding that "it lacked, for example, the racial component that is typical of fascism."[15] In fact, the influence of *völkisch* ideology in the Weimar Republic is a complicated topic and did not lead all Germans who might have been attracted to a "healthy nationalism" to racialism and exclusion.[16] In his excellent study on *völkisch* ideology, Roderick Stack-

---

us Germans . . . It has to do with a specific, closed blood relationship. Race is not already *Volk*, the biological unity is not already historical unity. But the unity of race in a significant sense and its protection is an essential condition for the formation and preservation of the *Volk*" (Ericksen, *Theologians Under Hitler*, 106-107).

11. Green, "Pacifism and Tyrannicide," 33. Green does, however, recognize that Bonhoeffer speaks in a sermon from July 29, 1928, on the church of Christ inhabiting the world, but still believes he is not immune to *völkisch* sentiment (cf. *DBWE* 10, 3/8, 507, n. 4).

12. *DBWE* 10, 2/3, 371.

13. Rasmussen, *Dietrich Bonhoeffer: Reality and Resistance*, 100-101.

14. Tödt notes that Bonhoeffer's Barcelona lecture "Basic Questions on a Christian Ethic" is "often approached with uneasy and sad feelings, and occasionally also with apologetic attempts at exoneration" (*Authentic Faith*, 77).

15. Ibid., 118.

16. In 1926, for example, *Volksgemeinschaft* was being proclaimed by the

elberg distinguishes between the idealism captured in German Romanticism and the perversion that comes out of it as a political agenda, noting that one of the original intentions of *völkisch* ideology was "to consolidate national consciousness and transcend class conflict" (Bonhoeffer actually writes on the problem of internal strife in Germany at this time).[17] Woodruff D. Smith has also considered the complexities of *völkisch* ideology in the context of the *Nationalsozialistische Deutsche Arbeiterpartei*: "The new forms of conservative ideology that appeared in German politics during the Wilhelmian era have bedeviled historians for years, both because their relationship to Naziism (although obviously important) is not clear and because they appear to be a confusing welter of ideas, some congruent, some wildly inconsistent. Attempts to fit them all into a single category on the basis of their intellectual content have not been successful."[18]

Given his background, I would argue that Bonhoeffer was not intellectually divided in a short space of time between a nationalism that had not reached its radical potential and a fledging pacifism that constitutive of the ecumenical movement; rather his application of *Volk* imagery functioned as a *rhetorical* device that intentionally and strategically created a conflict of interest in those listening. This strategy was a characteristic of his enthusiasm for sermons that pushed the envelope as he tried to stir his congregation to hard thinking on spiritual matters.[19] Bonhoeffer, then,

---

government's press agency (prior to Hitler) as a means of unity, to recognize a common bond and fate for the whole German people and to promote a healthy nationalism (Verhey, *Spirit of 1914*, 216).

17. Stackelberg, *Idealism Debased*, 5.

18. Smith, *Ideological Origins of Nazi Imperialism*, 84.

19. The debate concerning this issue can be located in *DBWE* 10, 27, n. 130 (see also Bethge, *Dietrich Bonhoeffer: A Biography*, 111). Against the argument of Bonhoeffer's susceptibility to nationalistic fervor, I would suggest two incidental points of evidence from his work. In *Sanctorum Communio*, Bonhoeffer's discussion on the human race comes under the topic of original sin, and he specifically avoids using the word *Rasse* for race, which has connotations of biological priority, and instead uses the word *Geschlecht* to indicate the whole of humanity. Final editing of this work comes at the time of Barcelona. Secondly, Bonhoeffer speaks derisively that Pastor Fritz Olbricht's

appears to be encouraging his congregation toward the hard task of ethical reflection. Bethge writes, "People were to be confronted and excited, shaken out of their complacency and won over."[20] Just as Bonhoeffer was not divided between nationalism and ecumenism, I likewise find it doubtful that in the space of a single sermon Bonhoeffer places himself in contradiction, especially given the time, attention, and thought he reportedly put into his sermons. At the beginning of the passage, Bonhoeffer asks, "Indeed, is not my enemy just as much my neighbor as is my biological brother? Is not the great deed of Christianity precisely that it leveled these distinctions, through the powerful notion of universal brotherhood?" Bonhoeffer's "neighbor" here is none other than the enemy. But now Bonhoeffer comes to the point of the passage: "If ever I find myself in the distressing situation of having to decide whether to expose my biological brother, my biological mother, to the hand of the attacker, or to raise my own hand against the enemy, then the moment itself will doubtless tell me which of these two is and must be my neighbor, including before the eyes of God." Surely, here the ethical moment makes no provision for premeditation. So why does Bonhoeffer arrive at the recommendation to defend his kin? The question of whether Bonhoeffer is recommending a specific course of action that would likewise apply in all examples of this kind of dilemma or whether he is working out an ethical solution for the purpose of demonstrating a concrete act of ethical decision making in his preaching has been ignored in the literature.[21]

---

reading materials consist of nationalistic materials in Barcelona, which continue to perpetrate a romantic nostalgia for Germany. An observation closely related to the depiction of tension between Bonhoeffer's roles as theologian and pastor in Barcelona comes from Zimmerman, who recalls how Bonhoeffer was overlooked in his own father's church (prior to his leaving for London) due to an intellectual headiness that the leadership feared would not resonate with the congregation ("Years in Berlin," 64).

20. Bethge, *Dietrich Bonhoeffer: A Biography*, 111.

21. The situational dilemma in Bonhoeffer's writing is raised in dialogical recourse to the normative explanation he is refusing. This theme is fairly consistent and reaches as far back to Barcelona and through to *Ethics*. An example of this appears in his thoughts on suicide (*Selbstmord*) in *Ethics*. He poses the reasons how a person who takes his own life stands in judgment for sin before

113

However, considering Bonhoeffer's heavy emphasis on concretion, it would be an unusual move for Bonhoeffer to offer a universal principle as a solution for a concrete decision. Furthermore, if the argument is that loyalty to one's people will invariably derive from the moment, the solution completely ignores the previous question Bonhoeffer poses, and in fact diminishes the importance of the decision because the same is already decided *before* the moment arrives. Can the question posed by Bonhoeffer reconcile itself to the answer in a way that has otherwise not been suggested? I believe this possible.

Bonhoeffer wants to emphasize that the moment should not find a person indecisive, but rather that one must decide according to what he believes is God's truth. The point of Bonhoeffer's rhetorical example is not that one chooses his kin but rather *how* one gets to that decision. Only then can the decision be justified, which Bonhoeffer in fact demonstrates by explaining the criteria that accompanies the decision to show that it lacks arbitrariness. Of course for some of the reasons previously mentioned that pertain to the complexity of *Volk* ideology, the selection of this decision does not carry with it the stigma that becomes an issue after 1933. Furthermore, that this passage should be read *rhetorically* is suggested by a comparison of Rasmussen's interview with Otto Dudzus, in which he writes of Bonhoeffer's Fanö sermon: "Otto Dudzus, also at Fanö . . . adds the important point that Bonhoeffer's language lacking 'ifs,' 'whens,' 'hows,' and other qualifiers of absolute pacifism, was the language of proclamation and demand, of grace and its claims. There is a very good reason, for the Fanö address was a sermon."[22] Although the formal denomination between Barcelona and Fanö is the difference between a lecture and a sermon, the Barcelona "lecture" is hardly of the academic sort but

---

God (a normative ethical claim). But then he shows that the situation invites other Christian actions that come into direct conflict with the demand to preserve his own life, for example, dying for a friend. In this, he resolves that a third way points us in the direction of truth. One must answer to God alone. The principle and the situation are altogether secondary and cannot represent the ground where one finds the truth he needs to make a decision.

22. Rasmussen, *Dietrich Bonhoeffer: Reality and Resistance*, 105.

was part of a series of topics addressed to interested laity within the congregation. It is difficult to see how the boldness with which Bonhoeffer raises the issue of loyalty to his *Volk* is not similar to the "language of proclamation" we find in Fanö. While Bethge writes that Bonhoeffer would never again make such a statement as "love for my people will . . . sanctify war," this may only have occurred because Bonhoeffer became aware that *völkisch ideology* was moving further away from a summons to cultural consciousness and was instead being gradually propagandized into a racially destructive ideology in the period immediately following. Political, not theological, change appears to have contributed to a responsible change in emphasis.[23]

Furthermore, Bonhoeffer's congregation in Barcelona was German with patriotic sensitivities. As Robertson writes of the congregation, they "looked forward to the time when they could return to a homeland much as they had left it."[24] *Völkisch* ideology is therefore introduced with emotive force to raise an ethical dilemma at the expense of a nostalgic expatriate audience who would recognize the concept intuitively but who might not have considered in themselves the ability to analyze how and under what conditions such a decision could be taken up in faith. One considers whether Bonhoeffer was able to create pause in his audience, who might have otherwise approached the question less reflectively had they been in the beer hall and not in the church.[25] Yet despite

23. Bethge, *Dietrich Bonhoeffer: A Biography*, 187–88. I would argue that such an interpretation fits Bonhoeffer's interpretive method, where Bethge stresses the change of circumstances as the primary filter of decision making.

24. Robertson, *The Shame and the Sacrifice*, 49–50.

25. Everything we know about Bonhoeffer from his letters and diary during this period contradicts a profile of a nationalistic thinker. His innate love for foreigners and culture, interest in Spanish and Muslim dialogue along with Catholic customs from the country is emphasized again and again. Bonhoeffer's refusal to keep to himself, even going so far as to select accommodations owned by Spanish women in hopes of helping him with his own study of the Spanish language, and his letter to his parents in which he fondly writes at the close of his time in Spain how it felt like home (January 28, 1929) are all strong indicators that his use of *völkische* ideology was an attempt at drawing in his audience and capturing their attention. In short, his very life betrays a

Bonhoeffer's attempt to create an enlightened church community during his stay in Barcelona, his efforts were most likely lost on an expatriate church community made up primarily of businessmen who were only interested in nostalgic representations of German church tradition and the comfort of familiar ritualism made possible by their pastors.[26]

The Ethical Collective Person

The identification of the ethical collective person (*Kollectivperson*) is essential for understanding Bonhoeffer's ethics.[27] The identity of this concept can actually be traced to Luther's own influence on Bonhoeffer's thinking, as well as Seeberg's influence over the writing of *Sanctorum Communio*. During his time in Barcelona, Bonhoeffer was busy editing his doctoral dissertation for publication, in which a section was dedicated to "Ethical Collective Persons." Here, Bonhoeffer wrote on sin as it applies to both individuals and the human race.[28] The section is of particular interest because Bonhoeffer's example of national destiny and war track with his comments from his Barcelona writings. As is the case in Barcelona, the question of whether *Volkstheologie* expresses itself in *Sanctorum Communio* haunts this section, to which Green affirmatively responds, "Bonhoeffer clearly did not yet consider his own statements on people [*Volk*], history, and war to be problematic."[29]

Since I have addressed the kind of *völkisch* ideology Bonhoeffer is being indicted with above, there is no need pursuing this line further. Here I want to pursue an understanding of the concept of the *Kollectivperson* through his examination of sin. Bonhoeffer

---

nationalistic reading of his words on almost every level.

26. The community seems not to have been too keen on Bonhoeffer's enthusiasm. He appears to have been discouraged by the bishop from starting too many programs that he would likely not be around to finish (Robertson, *The Shame and the Sacrifice*, 48).

27. Green, *Sociality of Christ and Humanity*, 70.

28. A more thorough analysis of sin and guilt is discussed below.

29. *DBWE* 1, 296.

believes that the proper interpretation of Christ's becoming human (*Menschwerdung*) cannot be abstracted from community. Where emphasis had been on the atoning work of Christ directed toward the individual who then enters the community, especially in Lutheranism, Bonhoeffer expresses the idea of Christ's redemptive mode directed to the community as a social category. First, Jesus redeems the sin of Adam individually. Redemption of sin is understood as the response to a condition of humanity's lost relationship with God.[30] If Adam's individual sin is redeemed individually, then his sin is no longer the point of contact for the conquering of the "sin curse" that comes by way of Christ. For Bonhoeffer, Adam's sin is something more. Like Barth, Bonhoeffer blurs the lines between an *ad hoc* original sin and sin as an existential condition of humanity's being. The importance of individual sin is that it is representative of the deeper fragmentation of the community. "In the sin of every man the common sinfulness of mankind is awakened."[31] What is "collective" about the sin of Adam is not that we share in its consequences by way of some doctrine of creationism or traducianism in that Adam supernaturally transfers its penalties upon us. We share in Adam's sin because he shares in ours. Bonhoeffer, like his contemporaries, analyzes sin as an ontological concept, its theological importance was in its binding individuals not simply to the community, but into the body of Christ, which represented a new orientation and new life. For reasons such as this, Bonhoeffer's awareness of the individual is always worked out in context to its socio-theological interpretation.

Green's *The Sociality of Christ and Humanity* offers important observations on the collective value of sin in Bonhoeffer's theology, and in particular the application of the *Kollectivperson* in the context of war. Bonhoeffer's elevation of the community into a kind of "superperson" is conditioned in the Hegelian thinking (*Geist*) of the time. The I–Thou relationship between God and humanity is

---

30. In this way, too, Bonhoeffer, perhaps without even knowing it, avoids traditional criticism of penal substitution models in which the idea of one innocent dying for all seemed inequitable and unjustified.

31. Green, *Sociality of Christ and Humanity*, 76.

for Bonhoeffer constitutive of all relationships, whether between individuals or individual and group, family, or nation.[32] Nevertheless—and here is where I see the difference with the perversion of *Volkstheologie* during this era—at no time does Bonhoeffer elevate community above the individual in a way that makes it inscrutable and unanswerable to the individuals in the community itself. What is important, as Green notes, is that "the very reason he applies to communities his own model of the human person is *to guarantee that they are understood to have the same ethical-historical character as the individual person*."[33] Here, where the concept of the *Kollectivperson* might have been perverted to capitalize on *völkisch* service to the state and efface the individual, Bonhoeffer remains committed to the individual who forms the community in the bonds of love through Christ. Bonhoeffer gives an example of this in a passage drawn from Genesis in which Abraham negotiates with God to spare Sodom and Gomorrah. The point is not that the mercy of God is myopically attuned to the salvation of one soul, but that on behalf of one righteous person, the community would be saved. Just as Christ acts on behalf of collective humanity and not simply for the individual, so individuals can act on behalf of the community. The example itself prefigures Bonhoeffer's own resistance activity and his frustration with the failing support of the Confessing Church.

Bonhoeffer continues, "There is a will of God with a people just as with individuals. Where a people, submitting in conscience to God's will, goes to war in order to fulfill its historical purpose and mission in the world—though entering fully into the ambiguity of human sinful action—it knows it has been called upon by God, that history is to be made; here war is no longer murder."[34]

32. Ibid., 67.

33. Ibid., 70. In another helpful note, Green writes, "In *Sanctorum Communio* he argued that the church as the new humanity was real and complete as an ontological reality in Christ, and that its social and temporal actualization resulted from the action of the Holy Spirit, who enables individuals to appropriate the new humanity in personal faith (*DBWE* 6, 7 in reference to *DBWE* 1, 141–47, 157–61).

34. *DBWE* 1, 119. Interestingly, a change occurs between the dissertation

Bonhoeffer and the Question of Murder

At the time this was written, Germany had recently lost the first war and was still suffering under the Treaty of Versailles. Hitler had not yet taken power, nor was he calling for war or speaking in any official capacity about the destiny of Germany. If this statement is linked to a militant *völkisch* ideology, it appears incredibly out of touch with reality: Bonhoeffer gives every indication he is aware that Germany did not succeed in the war, but failed. Rather, statements coming from Bonhoeffer at this time support the view that Germany was under the judgment of God. What does remain in this statement is the continual care with which Bonhoeffer objects to social categories of right and wrong that cannot be grounded in God.

I think there are two more important points that can be derived from this section: (1) The example of war was familiar and heartbreaking to a German audience. The comment demonstrates the power of community moving with common purpose, although with unknown results. (2) The fact that Bonhoeffer mentions the ambiguous nature of human sinful action suggests that his readers had intimate knowledge of war, whether this meant being in war, or had suffered the loss of family and friends to war. Germany was shamed and disgraced, and yet Bonhoeffer might have been implying that faithfulness was more important than success. This is all the more ironic considering Bonhoeffer sees Germany's defeat as a result of the sin and swollen pride of the German people.

What does Bonhoeffer mean then that war is no longer murder? Clearly, he is working in the confidence of his method. It is only in the ambiguity of good and evil that one goes *beyond good and evil* and clings to God. By human standards, war is murder. Murder is sin. Yet, God calls his people to any number of actions within the ever-changing motion of history, making it impossible

---

and publication manuscripts, and appears to have been prompted by correspondence with Seeberg. Bonhoeffer's original manuscript contained the statement "war is more than murder" (SC-A) to which Seeberg responds "ambiguous!" The publication manuscript (SC-B) replaces the offending statement with "war is no longer murder." Around this time, in his lecture on "Basic Questions of a Christian Ethic," Bonhoeffer waxes critical against the problematic nature of the commandment, not murder *per se* (see *DBWE* 10, 2/3, 270).

to measure the moral efficacy of any action based upon principles of proper conduct that transcend the historically bound actions wherein they manifest. Furthermore, the influence of his Barcelona sermon on Christian ethics is felt in the phrase, "the ambiguity of human sinful action," which until this point in his analysis of sin in the section "Ethical Collective Persons" of his dissertation had been nonexistent, but now squares with the example of war from his sermon. On July 20, 1944, after the failed attempt on Hitler's life, Bonhoeffer wrote to Bethge that "one only learns to have faith by living in the full this-worldliness of life."[35] Rather than offering a new theological insight, this haunting sentence recalls a consistent dimension of Bonhoeffer's ethics as it takes on specific concrete form in his own life.

Murder[36]

One of Bonhoeffer's most relevant reflections on the question of murder is found in *Discipleship*. Here, states Rasmussen, murder is considered an absolute boundary that cannot be permitted.[37] *Discipleship* is indeed a reaction to the specific concrete activity, at which time, was "the increasing Nazi mistreatment and murder of the Jews."[38] In his section entitled "Kindred," Bonhoeffer provides commentary to Matthew 5:21–26. In his rejection of murder, Jesus is not making an absolute declarative statement in the same way one approaches the prohibition contained within the Mosaic law. Jesus' words come to us as "But I say to you." Bonhoeffer sees this not as inviolable law taking the place of another inviolable law. For this reason, Bonhoeffer does not believe Jesus is rhetorically con-

---

35. *DBWE* 8, 4/178, 486.

36. I choose this word intentionally. Other scholars prefer tyrannicide, killing, or assassination, but these seem an attempt to sanctify an act which Bonhoeffer continually viewed in close connection to his broader concepts of sin and guilt.

37. Rasmussen, *Dietrich Bonhoeffer: Reality and Resistance*, 50. But note that it is an absolute boundary in view of the current commandment.

38. *DBWE* 4, 121, n. 85.

sistent with the rabbis in so far as "an exchange of opinion versus opinion" is opening up (It is possible Bonhoeffer imagines here the she'elah / teshuvah form of rabbinic dialectics on Jewish *halakhah*). Rather, here exists Christ as expressed authority as both the speaker and that which is spoken (i.e., the word *from* God and the Word *of* God) who is the "law of God." Christ's ethical being transcends the juridical and *halakhic* notion of the community under Mosaic law, insofar as he is the medium through which the interpretation of murder is to be understood. Jesus does not confine the act of murder to physical violence, but rather claims it to be, as Bonhoeffer interprets, "an aim *in hatred* to destroy another's internal and external existence."[39] That Bonhoeffer decontextualizes the commandment as a prohibition directed against physical violence only to recontextualize murder as annihilation is clearly in keeping with his methodological approach.[40] The one who responds to the commandment "Thou shalt not kill" is obliged first to seek out Christ, the law of God, in faith. The plain sense is therefore stripped of its dominion, which then opens up the interesting possibility (and one which will have meaning for Bonhoeffer later) that the physical taking of a life may be permissible where it can be wrested from annihilation. Bonhoeffer in fact achieves this by conceptualizing Hitler's murder as an act that puts away an evil against the humanity that is taken up in the work of creation by God and affirmed in the person of Christ.[41]

It is important to caution that Bonhoeffer's move to assist in the murder of Hitler is undertaken as an intellectual exercise, and neither did he make an easy transition from observer to conspirator. Bonhoeffer could not stand in the action and be entirely unaffected by the realities he helped enable. That Bonhoeffer suffered over the question of his role in the murder of Hitler is undeniable.

39. My emphasis.

40. For an interesting argument on the use of annihilation (*l'khalotam*) as a qualitative and quantitative action in the context of the massive loss of life in the Holocaust, see Halivni, *Breaking the Tablets: Jewish Theology After the Shoah* (Rowman & Littlefield Publishers, Inc., 2007).

41. Rasmussen, *Dietrich Bonhoeffer: Reality and Resistance*, 139.

Schlingensiepen summarizes: "He wondered whether someone who had helped plot to kill another human being should still be allowed to administer Holy Communion. Today we can hardly imagine the scruples that the conspirators had to overcome." Yet Schlingensiepen adds this note: "That Bonhoeffer had fought his way to clear answers was the fruit of his work on the *Ethics* . . ."[42]

The conflict that Bonhoeffer "suffered" does not appear to be over whether a change in his theological orientation is necessary, thus contradicting his previous work; nor is this conflict cause to reconsider a more normative approach to ethics and one more restricted to the letter of the law, which would require him to re-examine the nature of good and evil. Rather, this conflict pushes Bonhoeffer to discover how he might address the *perception* and *social stigma* of evil and treachery committed at his hand. Here, the social pressures are stronger (and more subtle) than the theological challenges that might betray his established body of work. One must not consider this a particular weakness but rather the evidence of a person doing the hard task of ethics in trying times when an action could create unforgivable consequences.[43]

In one thinly veiled autobiographical reflection on ethical behavior written during the time of the conspiracy, Bonhoeffer writes on criticism with regard to the responsible man as opposed to the cowardly conformist:

> Those, however, who take their stand in the world in their *very own freedom*, who value the necessary action more highly than their own untarnished conscience and reputation, who are prepared to sacrifice a barren principle to a fruitful compromise or a barren wisdom of the middle way to a fruitful radicalism, should take heed lest precisely their presumed freedom ultimately cause them to fall. They will easily consent to the bad, knowing full well that it is bad, in order to prevent the worse, and no longer be able to recognize that precisely the worse

---

42. Schlingensiepen, *Dietrich Bonhoeffer, 1906–1945*, 274.
43. *DBWE* 12, 1/86, 159.

Bonhoeffer and the Question of Murder

choice they wish to avoid may be the better one. Here lies the raw material of tragedy."[44]

The question of "worse choice" versus the "bad choice," I would argue is not an ethical qualification. But in keeping with the argument in this section of *Ethics* against those who "weigh sins," it would seem that Bonhoeffer is addressing social distinctions, and not offering theological insights, when he writes:

> The contours are sharply drawn . . . One sin is not like another. They have different weights. There are heavier and lighter sins. Falling away [*Abfall*] is far more serious than falling down [*Fall*]. The most brilliant virtues of the apostates are as dark as night compared with the darkest weaknesses of the faithful."[45]

During the early stages of Bonhoeffer's resistance participation, he was questioned directly on the issue of murdering Hitler. When asked by his brother-in-law, Dohnanyi, if it is wrong for a Christian to murder another, Bonhoeffer tells him that "murder is still murder." This is no direct answer to Dohnanyi's question of right or wrongdoing.[46] However, Bonhoeffer was reported to say that Hitler's murder was one of necessity and that one must be prepared to take the guilt of *this* sin on himself. Here there is no absolute condemnation of the act, only the warning of being *prepared* to bear this act as sin.[47] Behind this response is the developing theology in *Ethics*, where Bonhoeffer analyzes the nature of guilt as an act of responsibility, not of dishonor. It must be remembered

---

44. *DBWE* 6, 79–80.

45. Ibid., 77.

46. This anecdote has fed into the rather oversimplified relationship between sin and murder in Bonhoeffer. For example, Weikart approvingly quoting Schlingensiepen states, "Bonhoeffer recognized that killing Hitler would be murder and thus sinful, but he nonetheless thought it the most responsible course of action" (Weikart, "So Many Different Bonhoeffers," 76).

47. Although he understands Bonhoeffer's commitment to the concrete command, Weikart raises this point as an example of the ethical problem he thinks Bonhoeffer is creating (Weikart, *The Myth of Dietrich Bonhoeffer: Is His Theology Evangelical?*, 105).

that Schlingensiepen's own summary of the conversation is one of biography and does not account for the subtle theological associations that, in my analysis, bar a contradiction of this rank as an all too unrefined aberration for a theologian of Bonhoeffer's quality.

Another incident in the oral tradition recalled by Wolf-Dieter Zimmermann regards a conversation between the conspirators that took place in Zimmermann's own home in November 1942. Here, Werner von Haeften, who was executed shortly after the failed July 20, 1944 plot against Hitler, asked Bonhoeffer whether he "should" and "may" shoot Hitler.[48] Von Haeften had unparalleled access to Hitler at the time and felt a personal responsibility to go through with the act. Bonhoeffer's advice, as Zimmerman recalls, diminished the value of divine permission for a sinful act. Instead, Bonhoeffer was concerned with the ability of the plan to be executed.[49] Yet, as he did address the question of guilt, he indicated that nobody acting responsibly can escape it and that a person would experience guilt no matter which way he chose.[50]

Then there is the testimony provided by Emmi Bonhoeffer, Dietrich's sister-in-law, who recalled the following conversation with him:

> I remember I asked him, "How's that with you Christians? You will not kill but that another one does it you agree and you are glad about?" And then he said, "One shouldn't be glad about [it], but I understand what you mean. It is out of the question that a Christian ask someone else to do the dirty work so that he can keep his own hands clean.* If one sees that something needs to be done then one must be prepared to do it, whether one is a Christian or not. If one sees the task as necessary according to one's own conscience. Later on he used another example. He said, if I see that a madman is driving a car into a group of innocent bystanders then I as

---

48. Retter, *Theological-Political Resistance: the Role of Dietrich Bonhoeffer and Hans-Bernd von Haeften in the German Resistance Against Hitler*, 76. Retter notes a similar conversation that von Haeften has with his brother.

49. Rasmussen, *Dietrich Bonhoeffer: Reality and Resistance*, 140–141.

50. Dramm, *Dietrich Bonhoeffer and the Resistance*, 213–14.

Bonhoeffer and the Question of Murder

a Christian cannot simply wait for the catastrophe and comfort the wounded and bury the dead. I must try to wrest the steering wheel out of the hands of the driver.[51]

Tyannicide

What I want to analyze briefly in this section is whether Bonhoeffer's justification for the killing of Hitler is properly located in the tradition of tyrannicide or within his own methodology.[52] The consequence being that if justification is located in his methodology, then what does that mean for an appeal to the tradition, or *vice versa*?

In defining the type of plot against Hitler, Green asserts that Bonhoeffer was involved in tyrannicide, not assassination or murder as "is frequently and carelessly done in discussions of Bonhoeffer."[53] The tradition of tyrannicide is not only a political one but is also of the church. As early as 1415, the Council of Constance had convened to discuss the issue brought to bear by the murder of the Duke of Orleans. When a statement of resolution was finally published, it was ambiguous enough to prohibit the murder of a legitimate ruler but *allow* for the murder of a usurper or *tyrannus absque titulo*.[54] The question of how to define these

51. Boehlke and Drake, *Dietrich Bonhoeffer: Memories and Perspectives*. From the asterisk going forward, Emmi Bonhoeffer begins to speak in German and the text is translated by an interpreter.

52. While I was not able to evaluate fully the reading of Bonhoeffer advanced by Mark Thiessen Nation, Anthony G. Siegrist, and Daniel P. Umbel, their recent work on Bonhoeffer discusses his relationship to tyrannicide and peacemaking (*Bonhoeffer the Assassin? Challenging the Myth, Recovering his Call to Peacemaking*, 2013).

53. Green, "Pacifism and Tyrannicide," 41. A thoroughgoing attempt to identify Bonhoeffer's action with tyrannicide has not been unanimously accepted by other Bonhoeffer scholars. For example, Rasmussen does not entirely distinguish assassination from tyrannicide (*Dietrich Bonhoeffer: Reality and Resistance*, 131). Dramm calls Bonhoeffer's action a "political murder" and likewise refers to it as assassination (*Dietrich Bonhoeffer and the Resistance*, 214).

54. Lewy, "Secret Papal Brief," 320.

conditions unfortunately is never spelled out there, and as such it created an exception. As one author noted, "There were those within the church who conspired against the lives of sovereigns."[55] Bonhoeffer's connection to this tradition from within the church is advanced by Karl Barth, and it seems to me that Barth's interpretation is primarily responsible for the ideological separation of tyrannicide and murder: "Is it really murder, or is it an act of loyalty commanded *in extremis*, and therefore not murder? Might it not be that on occasion certain men not only may but must undertake it?"[56]

Bonhoeffer himself says nothing of a direct nature about tyrannicide in his written works.[57] Green admits this much, but he asserts that the concept is disguised.[58] Of course, there was good reason for concealing overt threats directed at the life of the Führer, first and foremost being that any form of threat could have resulted in a death sentence for the one involved. This rationale cannot therefore be *the* supporting defense for tyrannicide because it could be asserted that Bonhoeffer practiced a general carefulness for fear of implicating himself or others at this time.

What is interesting, however, is that while Green notes the connection of tyrannicide to a political tradition, he does not link what he believes is Bonhoeffer's approval to the tradition but to Bonhoeffer's own ethics, in which the free responsible action of an individual might lead to such confrontation. This free responsible action, Green rightly points out, requires the rejection of principles. Tyrannicide would not be considered a principle of ethical protocol because it remains grounded in Bonhoeffer's Christological ethics. If then Bonhoeffer's knowledge of tradition is not the controlling influence but his ethics *is* a particular problem is created.

---

55. Ibid., 323.

56. Barth, *Church Dogmatics*, 3.4:449.

57. Though there is no direct quote linking this logic to Bonhoeffer's own words, among scholars like Green and Rasmussen, tyrannicide for Bonhoeffer constitutes an action in which the physical taking of a life is permissible despite its characteristic similarity with murder.

58. Green, "Pacifism and Tyrannicide," 42.

Bonhoeffer and the Question of Murder

Despite Green's assertion of Bonhoeffer's rejection of principles, the danger of identifying tyrannicide as a form of murder is so bound to a particular response and special circumstance that it is hard to see exactly how tyrannicide remains interpretatively open to the free responsible action of the doer; whereas murder, at least in Bonhoeffer's earlier description in *Discipleship*, is constituted by multiple responses and is not limited to the physical act. Murder can be defined therefore by the individual working within a given context where annihilation of life is at issue. But tyrannicide, I would argue, is not afforded the same flexibility. This seems to me a good reason to dispense with semantics so that we may call it what it is: murder.

Secondly, scholarly support for tyrannicide is incidental at best. Green points to a lone passage in which Bonhoeffer calls Hitler the "tyrannical despiser of humanity."[59] Despite the use of this phrase to demonstrate tyrannicide as a live option because of the modifying descriptor assigned to Hitler in the use of this phrase, we have scant evidence (see above) for a formal theological response in the literature that would connect Bonhoeffer's lone phrase to any sort of coordinate action. Neither do we have evidentiary warrant to assert that the phrase he associates with Hitler infers within its range of meaning, the need for a moral response specifically aimed at addressing tyrannicide. There is simply no way to secure an acknowledgement in the Western theological tradition known to Bonhoeffer nor in his own writing of the very specific action of tyrannicide, and neither can we due to the nature of the censorship he was facing.

Thirdly, Green's support of tyrannicide as being the proper filter for understanding Bonhoeffer's work in the conspiracy is an argument from necessity in which "the very fundamentals of human life are at stake."[60] Bonhoeffer too spoke of necessity at this time, but it was a necessity that remained as much a question of murder (as my previous examples demonstrate) as Green believes it to be associated with a formal understanding of tyrannicide.

59. Ibid. (cf. *DBWE* 6, 85-87).
60. Ibid.

What seems at work behind Green's analysis is a rejection of vigilante responses that drives his attempt at a more succinct expansion of the concept, one which invariably includes murder as the action of "an individual acting on a self-appointed mission."[61]

This disagreement would only be semantic if it were not for Green's attempt to distinguish different types of killing. The fact that tyrannicide is controlled within the narrow window of a possible permission that comes from Reformation thinking is not very helpful here. At the same time, I want to stress that this is not an attempt to abstract the principle of murder from tyrannicide, but to keep tyrannicide from becoming abstract, remembering that for Bonhoeffer abstract ethical decision making is not just an appeal to idealism but is also antihistorical when it is applied without respect for historical peculiarity. This is why Bonhoeffer is careful not to associate murder absolutely with physical killing but rather in the injunction against the annihilation of another within the sociological framework of the community. It seems to me that the same cannot be said for a formal appeal to tyrannicide, where very specific criteria emerge in finding the basis of interpretation. It is not without relevance then that Bonhoeffer's main body of writings rejects qualitative distinctions between war and murder.

As I mentioned at the beginning of this section, tyrannicide appears to me as an apologetic attempt to curtail the horror of murder, which has precisely the opposite effect that Bonhoeffer would anticipate when one is open to the potential for personal loss that comes with responsible action. Such a distinction is an attempt to absolve, much like the case Zimmerman recalls in which von Haeften expresses his own concerns to Bonhoeffer. Tyrannicide as a charge diminishes the stigma of murder in favor of a more acceptable and legally binding definition, and remains problematic to Bonhoeffer's own ethical methodology as a dynamic response in the concrete.

---

61. Ibid., 41.

Bonhoeffer and the Question of Murder

Free Responsibility

In chapter 2, I discussed freedom and the role it plays in Bonhoeffer's concept of obedience. There we saw that "obedience to the trustworthiness of the person of Christ comes with the experience of freedom."[62] Emphasis was on a freedom from good and evil to engender simple obedience to Christ. Now, within the context of *Ethics*, the role of freedom in the language of obedience is gradually given greater emphasis in the concept of responsibility (*Verantwortung*).

The richness of the concept of responsibility in Bonhoeffer's ethics is not a decided matter in Bonhoeffer scholarship. For example, unlike Rasmussen who finds Bonhoeffer's emphasis on responsibility a move away from Christian exclusivism as it drives toward the goal of synthesizing the secular with the sacred, Wannenwetsch sees responsibility as a move that projects away from the individual's interiority with the goal of entering into an even deeper relationship with Christ.[63]

Though the concept of responsibility is often appropriated with attention to Bonhoeffer's later period, it does in fact key into concepts from his early work. One finds examples in *Creation and Fall* that prefigure into responsible living.

> The life that God gave to humankind is not simply part of the make-up [*eine Beschaffenheit*], a *qualitas*, of humankind; instead it is something given to humankind only in terms of its whole human existence. Human beings have life from God and *before* God. They receive it; they receive it, however, not as animals but as human beings. They possess it in their obedience, in their innocence, in their ignorance; that is, they possess it in their freedom.[64]

De Gruchy writes that it is here where the topic of freedom is introduced with regard to the freedom of humans to rule

62. Krötke, "Dietrich Bonhoeffer and Martin Luther," 75.
63. Wannenwetsch, "'Responsible Living or 'Responsible Self'?," 138–39.
64. *DBWE* 3, 84.

responsibly, that the subject "anticipates much of what Bonhoeffer was to write later in the manuscripts for his *Ethics*."⁶⁵ The consistency with which Bonhoeffer is able to negotiate freedom through to his *Ethics* is noted by Brocker, who points out the similarity of the concept here and Bonhoeffer's 1941 critique of William Paton's *The Church and the New Order*, which Bonhoeffer found promising for the reconstruction of a post-war Germany. Here Bonhoeffer explains the direction of this freedom:

> *Das Freisein von etwas erfährt seine Erfüllung erst in dem Freisein für etwas. Freisein allein um des Freiseins willen aber führt zur Anarchie. Freiheit bedeutet biblisch: frei sein fur den Dienst an Gott und am Nächsten, frei sein für den Gehorsam gegen die Gebote Gottes. Das setzt voraus: frei sein von jedem inneren und äuseren Zwang, der uns an diesem Dienst hindert.*⁶⁶

"Bonhoeffer's decision to take part in the conspiracy to assassinate Hitler was embedded in his concept of *Verantwortung*, a judgment that this course of action would lead to the end of his rule, an action for which he accepted the responsibility and the personal guilt."⁶⁷ Responsibility took on more substantive dimensions when Bonhoeffer presented it as a topic in a meeting with Karl Barth in September, 1941 to be worked by theologians of the Confessing church.⁶⁸ According to Wannenwetsch, Barth, like Bonhoeffer, had a broad view of responsibility that transcended the limitations of traditional ethical discourse to encompass the whole of human existence. Where freedom had been emphasized in service to obedience, responsibility proved that freedom and obedience belonged to a broader theological conversation that

---

65. Ibid., 11.

66. "Being free from something is experienced only in being free for something. Being free solely in order to be free, however, leads to anarchy. Freedom means, biblically, to be free for service to God and to one's neighbor; free for obedience against (*DBWE* 16, 532 renders this "obedience to") the commands of God. This presupposes to be free from each inner and outer pressure that hinders us in our service" (*DBW* 16:540; cf. *DBWE* 3, 67).

67. Blackburn, *Dietrich Bonhoeffer and Simone Weil*, 232.

68. Wannenwetsch, "Responsible Living or 'Responsible Self'?," 129.

Bonhoeffer sought to move beyond the restrictive boundaries of the church. The benefit of Bonhoeffer's Christological exposition of Genesis further illumined the truth of Christ's *Menschwerdung* as a reality-encompassing event that when filtered through the "lost world" of Genesis revealed the foundation for the greater truth of Christ's dominion and invited humans to redress their theological participation in the world. With Reich ideology pressuring the church into subservience to State activity, freedom for Bonhoeffer would have to be spoken of with regard to the responsible action that happened not only among the faithful, but within the civil sphere as well, which I contend he does without sacrificing any significant ethical insight.[69] Despite responsibility's greater dominion over the world, it was also a call to genuine humanity, and not merely a call to action (*Handeln*). Where responsibility was to be understood as the measure of one's entire being, Bonhoeffer could still talk about responding to the commandment of God in the concrete, which had already been attached to his Christology as one's submission to Christ.[70] Without this understanding of freedom's role in responsibility, Bonhoeffer contends, neither can exist independently.[71] Such an insight can also be found in *Creation and Fall* where Bonhoeffer points to freedom not as a freedom *from* but *for* the world.[72] But then freedom is only a short inference to responsibility. These earlier developments may have led Bonhoeffer to assert in his *Ethics*: "*Verantwortung und Freiheit sind einander korrespondierende Begriffe. Verantwortung setzt sachlich—nicht zeitlich—Freiheit voraus, wie Freiheit nur in der Verantwortung bestehen kann.*"[73]

Another reason for the introduction of responsibility can be read through Bonhoeffer's concern that obedience in the secular

69. Ibid.
70. *DBWE* 6, 381.
71. Ibid., 256.
72. *DBWE* 3, 66–67.
73. "Responsibility and freedom are mutually corresponding concepts. Responsibility presupposes objectively—not chronologically—freedom, such as freedom can exist only in responsibility" (my translation). (*DBW* 6:288).

and sacred sphere was often grasped prohibitively. Commenting on this, Bonhoeffer wrote that the German soldier lacked "free, responsible action, even against career and commission" because obedience was offered at the expense of freedom.[74] Bonhoeffer's call to responsible living attempted to extricate true obedience from the rank and file ethics that robbed the individual of freedom and subjugated him to the supremacy of the community.

Finally, Bonhoeffer ties the responsible act to representational being.[75] In this way, one is not only responsible for his stand on behalf of others but is also acting individually in such a way that he bears others in his action. Bonhoeffer asserts how the individual is never apart from the community, a commitment he maintained throughout his career as an ethical thinker: "Individuals do not act merely for themselves alone; each individual incorporates the selves of several people; perhaps even a very large number."[76] This double direction (the individual assumed into the community, and the community assumed into the individual) presumes the way in which representational action never exonerates the individual from others.

Sin and Guilt

How does one who performs any action in the name of God grapple with the problem of sin and guilt? The question took on new personal relevance as Bonhoeffer entered into conspiratorial knowledge and activities with the *Abwehr*. From his earliest writing, Bonhoeffer's insights are primarily an attempt to redefine traditional concepts of sin and guilt in the body of the community. As far as his methodology is concerned, sin is not simply the outcome of an action in defiance of a divine commandment, and likewise guilt is not the result of that sin.

---

74. *DBWE* 8, 41.
75. *DBWE* 6, 232.
76. Ibid., 221.

Bonhoeffer's early theological orientation to sin appears positive, and statements to this effect can be found in work from Barcelona as well as his academic work coming out of that time. In a letter to Walter Dreß from September 15, 1928, Bonhoeffer raises the question of how God may use sin to accomplish his will. Contrary to José J. Alemany's claim that Bonhoeffer did not resolve anything substantive from his time spent in Barcelona, Bonhoeffer admits in this letter that sin had always been theologically unambiguous for him, but now believes it not to be so easily resolved since his time spent in his pastoral duties in which he dealt with locals as well as his German congregation.[77] Bonhoeffer wonders openly how individuals might be assured in their sin that it is God's will as they see through it to Christ.[78] He paraphrases Luther's famous dictum: "*Esto peccator et pecca fortiter, sed fortius fide et gaude in Christo.*"

The suspicion that sin and guilt were not empirical phenomena but concepts that invited ontological analysis finds expression in *Sanctorum Communio*. Sin and guilt, Bonhoeffer says, reveal themselves as the basic structure of fallen humanity. Because of this Bonhoeffer strongly resists any analysis of personal sin and guilt as being the proper starting point for an understanding of the basic human condition. "Consciousness of guilt reveals to individuals their connection with all sinners."[79] In these early works, Bonhoeffer was attempting to define Adam's first original sin (*Erbsünde*) in the social context of the church as something that arises in the self-conscience shared by all members of the species. Bonhoeffer writes, "The concept of original sin as culpability [*Erbsünde als Schuld*] is correct only when it applies 'to the totality

---

77. "*Was Bonhoeffer in seinen Arbeiten dieser Epoche erkennen läßt, entstammt dem theologischen Gepäck, das sich in seinen erst kürzlich beendeten Studien angesammelt hatte, und zeigt keine substantiellen örtlichen Einflüsse, als er Spanien ein Jahr später verläßt*" (Alemany, "La Teologia Barcelonessa de Bonhoeffer," 1).

78. *DBWE* 10, 1/45a, 139–40.

79. *DBWE* 1, 121.

of the entire human race,' in which 'it cannot in similar fashion be the culpability of the individual.'"[80]

What appears to be informing Bonhoeffer's emphasis is wrapped up in his own rejection of normative ethical thinking. Primarily, it is his belief that the problem of sin traditionally held is always a problem of context and identification, of good and evil. As an example, the message taken from the story of Adam's fall is the fall of humanity (*Sündenfall*). The specific details of Adam's disobedience are notably absurd when adopted as a universal principle of conduct. With few exceptions, even the ancient authors recognized that the act of eating the apple was insufficient on its own merits as an example of sin long before it became an accepted exegetical truth.[81] It is the representative action (*stellvertretend Handeln*) that breaks relationship with God. Sin is then properly oriented to relationship rather than action.

The German notion of guilt (*Schuld*) used by Bonhoeffer has richer connotations than the English equivalent, and both Reinhard Krauss and Green note that *Schuld* is tied to the universal rather than individual.[82] Bonhoeffer goes further. Because individuation of Adam's sin is denied as exegetically important, since it is "impossible" to understand how individual sin leads to corporate guilt, Bonhoeffer is freed to make the claim in his later works that sin

80. Ibid., 113, n. 11.

81. Plenty of examples can be found in the pre-scientific world of the Post-Apostolic Fathers that relied upon fantastic narratives to explain theological truths, and yet analysis of the apple as an event-in-itself was generally excluded in favor of a deeper significance. One of the closest attempts at making sense of the apple's place in the Genesis story as a central motif and not simply as a marker of spiritual rebellion comes from Novatian, a leader in the Roman church. In his treatise *On the Jewish Meats*, he writes "from the beginning of things . . . the only food for the first men was fruit and the produce of the trees. For afterwards, man's sin transferred his need from the fruit-trees to the produce of the earth, when the very attitude of his body attested the condition of his conscience. For although innocency raised men up towards the heavens to pluck their food from the trees so long as they had a good conscience, yet sin, when committed, bent men down to the earth and to the ground to gather its grain" (Roberts, Donaldson, and Coxe, eds., *The Ante-Nicene Fathers, Volume V – Fathers of the Third Century*, 646).

82. *DBWE* 1, 114, n. 12.

and guilt are inextricably linked in the person of Christ who takes on *humanity* by taking on its guilt (*Schuldübernahme*). "The interweaving of the individual and the communal illuminates Bonhoeffer's account of sin, in which the culpability of the individual and all of humanity is closely connected."[83] Here one finds the context of all responsible action.[84]

By treating sin as an ontological concept, wherein one can talk about sin but not say anything of its phenomenal character, Bonhoeffer meant to underscore the primacy of our break with God in rejection of the particularity of abstraction. The actual phenomenon of sin remained within the world, but its identification rested on the individual who stands in relationship with God. At the height of his ecumenical work, Bonhoeffer also took up the question of sin with regard to the church. Bonhoeffer asserted that the church had far too long retreated into inaction when a precise knowledge of the concrete details had proven incomplete; and in the absence of clear biblical guidance, the church had excused itself from taking up the commandment of God as concrete action, in effect denying reality.

"If the church really has a commandment of God, it must proclaim it in the most definite form possible, from the fullest knowledge of the matter, and it must utter a summons to obedience."[85]

Moses has described Bonhoeffer's problem as an issue in which the full disclosure of the "realities of the world" was not possible; therefore it is only in the forgiveness of sins that the church can "pronounce fearlessly on the realities of the world."[86] The problem here is that Moses' analysis amounts to a tension between a knowledge of reality and an *ideal* knowledge of reality. For Bonhoeffer, a reality beyond what we know is never a question. The proper relationship of church and its knowledge of reality is not

---

83. Plant, *Bonhoeffer*, 66.
84. *DBWE* 6, 273.
85. *NRS*, 163.
86. Bonhoeffer calls this "knowledge of the matter" or "situation." This is akin to empirical data gathering. The "knowledge of reality" conveys a more holistic concept as humanity's engagement in the world. Neither is it epistemic knowledge in determining the nature of reality (*NRS*, 163).

the problem. The problem is that the church is unfaithful when it does not act with regard to reality (*Wirklichkeit*) as it is known, and the church *must* confidently assume in such cases where knowledge will always be incomplete the forgiveness of Christ.[87] Bonhoeffer's critique implies his own methodological rejection of the abstract commandment. First, abstraction divests the church of any personal risk because it expresses an inauthentic unity with the commandment that feigns ready accessibility and diminishes the role of faithfulness in the bonds of a genuine relationship with Christ. The church must risk speaking a concrete word to the world.[88]

But now Bonhoeffer brings us to the pivotal point. What happens when we act and, in doing so, sin? Bonhoeffer responds, "The church will recognise that it is blaspheming the name of God, erring and sinning, but it may speak thus in faith in the promise of the forgiveness of sins which applies also to the church."[89] Forgiveness of sin is not the individual fare of the believer that filters through a collective body of believers we call the church. Forgiveness of sin is the new collective life that constitutes the church. Access to and action in the world is only possible within the new life of forgiveness because the church is oriented to the world through forgiveness. Such explanations lay the groundwork in Bonhoeffer's *Ethics* for the merging of sacred and secular realities into *reality* as the believer's engagement in the world is no longer negotiated through the church or theocratic language that attempts a synergy between the moral language of religion with the political realm of time and space, but through Christ as the center of all things.[90]

---

87. Moses, *Reluctant Revolutionary*, 86. Bonhoeffer writes that "Reality is the sacrament of the command" so that where the knowledge of reality is "for the preaching of the command," it "rests on the forgiveness of sins" (cf. *NRS*, 164). Note, the translation error in *NRS*. I have aligned with current scholarship to replace "sacrament" with "command" (*Gebot*) (see Rasmussen, *Dietrich Bonhoeffer: Reality and Resistance*, 25, n. 48).

88. Woelfel, *Bonhoeffer's Theology*, 80.

89. *NRS*, 164.

90. While Rasmussen (*Dietrich Bonhoeffer: Reality and Resistance*, 24–25, n. 48) has noted that Bonhoeffer's Christocratic reality that comes in the *Ethics* is not yet formulated when Bonhoeffer was making his statements related

Bonhoeffer and the Question of Murder

As Bonhoeffer draws deeper into his own conspiracy activities, and the Confessing Church continues to disintegrate for various reasons, Bonhoeffer is once again led to recapture the place of the individual. In *Ethics*, he begins to expand on the topic of guilt as being the individual's responsible participation in humanity:

> Those who in acting responsibly take on guilt—which is inescapable for any responsible person—place this guilt on themselves, not on someone else; they stand up for it and take responsibility for it. They do so not out of a sacrilegious and reckless belief in their own power, but in the knowledge of being forced into this freedom and of their dependence on grace in its exercise.[91]

It is interesting that guilt still bears the anthropological mark that is inextricably bound to human ontology. Yet, the emphasis now is much more forceful with regard to the representational dimension of guilt. Bonhoeffer's analysis of Christ as being-for-others, which humanity itself takes on where Christ exists as the church, becomes integral for this emphasis. Bonhoeffer exceedingly turns to this dimension of guilt in which the Christological significance of representational being forms the ethical meaning for standing in guilt that is not one's own.

Bonhoeffer's increasing isolation also allows him to reflect on the sinfulness of his own actions. The meaning of this sinfulness, however, can only be understood with regard to responsible action that is always directed to others. This is why I cannot agree with Kelly and Nelson that ambiguous action is the precedent for "healthy guilt."[92] Guilt that is responsible or "healthy" must communicate itself while standing alongside and in place of others. It is

---

to the sacrament of reality and forgiveness in 1932, it should be noted that Rassmussen's own assertion that reality here is empirical data is made without explanation or qualification. It may be that these earlier intimations toward a Christocratic reality provide the necessary theological permission for Bonhoeffer to mature his thought toward its more expansive ends.

91. *DBWE* 6, 282.
92. Kelly and Nelson, *Cost of Moral Leadership*, 114.

one's determination to act responsibly despite the ambiguities that result from guilt, for the sake of others.

At this point in Bonhoeffer's writings, Rasmussen notes that Bonhoeffer makes little sense of the distinction between Christ "as *exemplum* for those who incur true guilt by acts of resistance that violate divine law, instead of being only the *exemplum* for forensic taking on of guilt." Rasmussen notes that "the passages in *Ethics* speak of guilt in very general terms. Yet Bonhoeffer's own experience of guilt is terrifyingly specific."[93] He asks if this guilt is "truly guilt," and points out that "the nest of issues around guilt and Christology is a very tangled one."[94] Unfortunately space here prevents an adequate discussion of this question.

In another place, Bonhoeffer does provide an example of responsibility in which the inference to guilt is not hard to detect. He writes that a father of a family "can no longer act as if he were merely an individual. In his own self, he incorporates the selves of those family members for whom he is responsible."[95] If the level of this commitment is as serious as I assert, then Bonhoeffer would have us believe that the father is not simply shamed by the actions of his family but enters into their guilt, and is prepared to accept the consequences. "Those who act responsibly take the given situation or context into account in their acting, not merely as raw material to be shaped by their ideas, but as contributing to forming the act itself."[96] When we ask what true guilt is we are implying the equally important question: What is guilt? Can there be guilt without the threat of consequence? If so, are we not now speaking to empathy? Suffering, however, whether physical or emotional, seems intrinsically tied to guilt, and Bonhoeffer speaks quite a bit to suffering. It appears that guilt is true for Bonhoeffer when it entails standing as Jesus stands in the place of the other, *as the other*, with every entitlement to the pain and punishment implied in that orientation, a fact that Bonhoeffer saw in Jesus' taking on

---

93. Rasmussen, *Dietrich Bonhoeffer: Reality and Resistance,* 54.
94. Ibid., 173.
95. *DBWE* 6, 221.
96. Ibid., 222.

humanity and which he saw in himself as a German who must stand for the German people.

This guilt is captured in Bonhoeffer's last poem from Tegel Prison. Gerard Th. Rothuizen writes, "The excessive feelings of guilt under which Bonhoeffer labored . . . can be interpreted as arising from his sense of solidarity with the sins of his people; here again a prophet, who in this case not deserting, allowed himself to be thrown overboard as a sin offering."[97] The poem itself was written in October 1944, when an opportunity to escape prison arose but which he rejected for fear that his family and friends would suffer repercussions.[98]

Here, Bonhoeffer imagines himself as Jonah. Unlike the biblical account, the sailors do not specifically seek out Jonah (*So flehten sie*). It is only Jonah who reveals himself (*Ich bin es!*). Jonah announces that he has sinned. The poem ends with Jonah being cast into the sea. Unlike the gospels where the story of Jonah is interpreted as a typology of Christ's death and resurrection, here Jonah is connected with an ethics of sin and guilt that may indeed rely on a formal distinction that Jonah is willing to share with all humanity. Although Jonah may be an example of the type of problem Rasmussen suspects—that Bonhoeffer at times does not make the best attempt to separate the burden of sin from the actual sin—Jonah's bold declaration of actual sin (*Ich sündigte vor Gott*), which when taken up in responsibility exonerates the righteous (*Der Fromme soll nicht mit dem Sünder enden!*), combines these two senses. Wannenwetsch notes that because the poem ends with Jonah being cast into the sea, "The theme . . . is not so much Jonah's salvation, but his willingness to die for the salvation of others."[99] I would add that a possible interpretation of the abrupt ending suggests that no further possibility exists in which Jonah can stand only in a formal position of representation. Furthermore, because we do not know whether or not Jonah is saved, such an ending aligns well with Bonhoeffer's

97. Rothuizen, "Who Am I? Bonhoeffer and Suicide," 178.
98. Rasmussen, *Dietrich Bonhoeffer: Reality and Resistance*, 199, n. 66.
99. Wannenwetsch, *Who Am I? Bonhoeffer's Theology through his Poetry*, 208.

own carefulness concerning how guilt and sin put an individual in a peculiar situation where faith is made all the more critical.

Green writes that as early as his work on *Sanctorum Communio*, Bonhoeffer's view on basic Christian concepts like sin had far-reaching influences on his theology.[100] In his chapter "Sin and Broken Community," Bonhoeffer addresses sin in the community and between individuals. Sin must be recognized as the unique inheritance of the entire human race (*Gesamtheit des ganzen Geschlechts*) and at the same time is manifest concretely. He rejects the notion of biological inheritance, precisely because it fails to account for all human variation (e.g., infants, the intellectually disabled) and has the effect of creating "ethically indifferent views of sin."[101] Instead, Bonhoeffer believes that original/individual sin is most appropriately expressed together. "The human being, by virtue of being an individual, is also the human race," so that "when, in the sinful act, the individual spirit [*Geist*] rises up against God ... the deed committed is at the same time *the deed of the human race in the individual person.*"[102] This leads Bonhoeffer to say that "all humanity falls with each sin." Even if this insight is not precisely an example of *Stellvertretung*, since human beings—and not Christ—sin and are oriented to sin, Bonhoeffer's interpretation of sin from the 1933 Berlin lectures on Christology might also be applied. In those lectures, Bonhoeffer addressed Christ's sinlessness, and concluded that behind this doctrine was the ethical dilemma

---

100. *DBWE* 1, 1.

101. Ibid., 114. Here, Bonhoeffer is closely tracking with Barth who, in his famous rebuttal of Emil Brunner, notes the problem of biological differentiation as an argument against humanity's ability to respond to God: "Is the revelation of God some kind of 'matter' to which man stands in some original relation because as man he has or even *is* the 'form' which enables him to take responsibility and make decisions in relation to various kinds of 'matter'? Surely all his rationality, responsibility and ability to make decisions might yet go hand in hand with complete impotency as regards *this* 'matter'! And this impotency might be the tribulation and affliction of those who, as far as human reason can see, possess neither reason, responsibility nor ability to make decisions: new-born children and idiots. Are they not children of Adam? Has Christ not died for them?" (Brunner and Barth, *Natural Theology*," 88–89).

102. *DBWE* 1, 115.

and material reality of uncovering the true nature of one's action. He further asserted that Jesus' actions were often mistaken for sin.[103] Nevertheless, the *Ich bin es* is close to the Jesus who speaks the "I am" in John's Gospel when he, too, is being sought. The pivotal point of Christ's embracing of humanity is that he became authentically "human." Like Jonah, Bonhoeffer's Jesus is permitted to say "I am a sinner" precisely because he stands within humanity. Standing in humanity is taking responsibility to stand in sin. Thus, *Stellvertretung* brings about other implications for a theology of sin. That an individual can act on behalf of a community even without the community's express knowledge or consent is a dimension in Bonhoeffer's Christology, and is also crucial to the conspiratorial conscience of those who opposed Hitler. Likewise, sin as the bearing of responsibility and sin as the suffering of misidentification because it rests in the prohibitive commandment rather than relationship are not only emphasized in his later writing and work but find basis in his earlier writings.

There is an interesting, if not autobiographical point, in *The Prayerbook of the Bible*. At the time of its publication in 1940, Bonhoeffer was deeply committed to resistance activities. In his examination of the Old Testament Psalms, he speaks on the concept of guilt as a situation that is only answered in Christ:

> If I am guilty, why does God not forgive me? If I am not guilty, why does God not end my torment and demonstrate my innocence to my enemies (Pss 38, 79, 44)? There is no theoretical answer to all these questions in the Psalms any more than in the New Testament. The only real answer is Jesus Christ. But this answer is already being sought in the Psalms. It is common to all of them that they cast every difficulty and tribulation [*Anfechtung*] upon God: "We can no longer bear them, take them away from us and bear them yourself, for you alone can handle suffering."[104]

---

103. *DBWE* 12, 2/12, 357.
104. *DBWE* 5, 170.

The question Bonhoeffer is answering is this: why does God not conform to the expectations of the supplicant? Against this backdrop it is important to note that a rejection of what is good and evil is implied in this passage, as well as the moral dimension of wrongful suffering, righteousness, and justice. The Psalmists do not leverage God's commandments to their defense against God. Bonhoeffer concludes that what is consistent in every case is that the supplicant always appeals to God rather than holding God to a principle of conduct. This interpretation remains tied to Bonhoeffer's relational, Christological ethics. We may once again look at the way forgiveness for Bonhoeffer is a lived reality and an orientation to Christ, rather than a response to a particular action. Bonhoeffer notes the following:

> There are fewer prayers for the forgiveness of sins in the Psalter than we expect. Most psalms presuppose complete certainty of the forgiveness of sins. That may surprise us. But even in the New Testament the same thing is true. Christian prayer is diminished and endangered when it revolves exclusively around the forgiveness of sins. *There is such a thing as confidently leaving sin behind for the sake of Jesus Christ.*[105]

But then why is there any guilt? If one is acting confidently in his relationship with God, should he not also be confident in his forgiveness? Bonhoeffer responds that suffering is still an inescapable anxiety and occurs because "God's ways are too difficult to grasp." This does indeed expose us to the possibility of guilt. How might one keep himself from the suffering of guilt while at the same time, in his responsible living, stand squarely in guilt? According to Bonhoeffer, this dilemma is answered in the person of Christ. This is not the Christ of Bonhoeffer's Berlin lectures whose sinlessness is contrasted to the ambiguity of human action, although this meaning is not wholly abandoned. Rather, by the time of the *Ethics*, the ambiguity of human action is emphasized within the problems traditionally attached to guilt. Christ is the one who declares us righteous and innocent so that the faithful can hold fast

---

105. Ibid., 171 (emphasis mine).

to their confession of faith despite all appearances to the contrary. Because Christ does this, Bonhoeffer asserts that one can answer, "I was blameless before [God], and I kept myself from guilt . . . If you test me, you will find no wickedness in me."[106] This emphasis on guilt as *Schuldübernahme*, especially in the sinless person of Christ, moves Bonhoeffer to conclude, "Those who act responsibly become guilty without sin."[107]

Most important, as Bonhoeffer speaks with regard to taking on sin and guilt, he never speaks from within the realm of deontological or formulaic ethical permissions, where exceptions must be pleaded at the expense of an impassable boundary condition of righteousness. Sin and guilt must always be interpreted in the deep waters of relationship with Christ.

Conclusion

Given the dramatic details of Bonhoeffer's life leading up to his death and the nature of his secret activities that caused him to question who he was and who others were, one expects there should be continued debates, monographs, papers, and interest surrounding Bonhoeffer's legacy and work. More than seventy years later, this has proven the case.

In this book, I have attempted to argue for a consistent approach in Bonhoeffer's theological reflections. Indeed, I have agreed with Bonhoeffer's own analysis of his self-consistency as being a trustworthy path for analyzing the body of his theological work. James H. Burtness's statement succinctly captures what I and others have argued, namely that "in order to get at the ethics of Dietrich Bonhoeffer it is necessary to locate those ethics across the entire spectrum of his life and work, and that the materials when examined yield an essentially consistent point of view."[108] In making the argument that the way to approach Bonhoeffer's

---

106. Ibid., 172.
107. *DBWE* 6, 282.
108. Burtness, *Shaping the Future*, 121.

understanding of the Christ-centered life is one that begins with ethical methodology, I have argued that the same methodology originates in Christ through whom we have recourse to ask the ethical question, and that the question maintains a form that remains consistent throughout Bonhoeffer's writings. For Bonhoeffer, Christ is our ethic *and* our methodology, which is precisely the abandonment of competing ethical methodologies grounded in socio-historical systems that force the question of right and wrong without the imposition of Christ.

I have also rejected the position that Bonhoeffer is replacing competing ethical systems with his own formal ethical Christology. Relational ethics focuses on the person of Christ in us and through us, but such focus does not entail that any attempt to examine the ways in which this relationship operates violates one's openness to Christ. This is possible because his ethical Christology begins with a question, rather than an answer. When Bonhoeffer asks "Who is Christ for us today?" we find in this statement a concise summary of the essential building blocks of this methodology: the *pro me* of Christ, the concretion of revelation, both Christ in the world and in our immediate circumstances, as well as the movement beyond deontic and ideal concepts of good and evil. To offer up such a question for reflection is not to suppose procedural directives that will lead to conclusive or repeatable results because such a question provides opportunity to reflect on the very person whose life in me and for me brings my own existence *as a response* into question.

In those sections of this book where I examined Bonhoeffer's engagement of peace and violence, I have argued that these concepts should not maintain a central position because they do not represent uniform or unambiguous starting points, but instead act as filters for the way Bonhoeffer does theology. The result is that Bonhoeffer does not make dramatic changes in the way he approaches his theology, despite the ever-deteriorating socio-political conditions in Germany. His methodology is Christological, and in order for an ethic to be Christological it must be built in relationship, rather than by way of conceptual spheres, theories of epistemology, or philosophical theology in general. This relationship exists beyond any social boundary of good and evil, and yet is buried within the world where questions of good and evil emerge rather than in the metaphysics about a reality that must be espoused first to be experienced.

Peace and violence in the ethics of Dietrich Bonhoeffer are not simply given to us by a precognitive or religious understanding of the terms. These concepts intersect, arrive, and take on changing forms within the ebb and flow of history. At times, emphases shift, coordinating theological language and arranging it in meaningful ways, but in ways that always meet the methodological demands of his Christological ethic, and always with regard to the way in which Bonhoeffer asks the ethical question. Attempts to read Bonhoeffer's theological development as a paradigmatic shift from peace to violence fail to reconcile his awareness of a world in crisis that must constantly reorient both itself and the concepts that sustain human engagement in openness to Christ where the processes of everyday life breakdown and provide no reliable guidance.

Bibliography

Alemany, José J. "La Teologia Barcelonessa de Bonhoeffer," Paper presented at the Second International Bonhoeffer Congress, Geneva, 1976. UTS Archives, Bonhoeffer Secondary Papers, Series 1B Box 1.
Bayer, Oswald. "Luther as Interpreter of Holy Scripture." In *The Cambridge Companion to Martin Luther*. Edited by Donald K. McKim, 73–85. Cambridge: Cambridge University Press, 2003.
Bagetto, Luca. "The Exemplification of Decision in Dietrich Bonhoeffer." In *Theology and Practice of Responsibility: Essays on Dietrich Bonhoeffer*. Edited by Wayne Whitson Floyd Jr. and Charles R. Marsh, 197–204. Valley Forge, Pa.: Trinity Press International, 1994.
Barth, Karl. *Church Dogmatics*. Edited by G. W. Bromiley and T. F. Torrance, Vol. 1.2. Peabody, MA: Hendrickson, 2010.
Barth, Karl. *Church Dogmatics*. Edited by G. W. Bromiley and T. F. Torrance, Vol. 2.2. Peabody, MA: Hendrickson, 2010.
Barth, Karl. *Church Dogmatics*. Edited by G. W. Bromiley and T. F. Torrance, Vol. 3.4. Peabody, MA: Hendrickson, 2010.
Barth, Karl. *The Epistle to the Romans*. 6th ed. Gütersloh: Oxford University Press, 1968.
Bendersky, Joseph W. *A History of Nazi Germany: 1919-1945*. Rowman & Littlefield, 2000.
Bentham, Jeremy. *Utilitarianism*. London: Progressive Publishing Co., 1890.
Bethge, Eberhard. "The Challenge of Dietrich Bonhoeffer's Life and Theology." In *World Come of Age*. Edited by Ronald Gregor Smith, 22–88. Philadelphia: Fortress, 1967.
Bethge, Eberhard. *Dietrich Bonhoeffer: A Biography*. Edited by Victoria J. Barnett. Minneapolis: Fortress, 2000.
Biggar, Nigel. *The Hastening That Waits: Karl Barth's Ethics*. Oxford: Clarendon, 2003.
Blackburn, Vivienne. *Dietrich Bonhoeffer and Simone Weil: A Study in Christian Responsiveness*. Switzerland: Peter Lang AG, 2004.

BIBLIOGRAPHY

Boehlke, Bain and Drake, Gerald, prods. *Dietrich Bonhoeffer: Memories and Perspectives*, DVD. Durban, South Africa: Video Vision Entertainment, 1996.

Bonhoeffer, Dietrich. *Christ the Center*. Edited by Eberhard Bethge. Translated by John Bowden. New York: Harper, 1966.

Bonhoeffer, Dietrich. *Dietrich Bonhoeffer Werke. Nachfolge*. Vol. 4. Edited by Eberhard Bethge, Ernst Feil, Christian Gremmels, Wolfgang Huber, Hans Pfeifer, Albrecht Schönherr, Heinz Eduard Tödt, Ilse Tödt. Gütersloh: Gütersloher Verlagshaus, 1992.

Bonhoeffer, Dietrich. *Dietrich Bonhoeffer Werke. Ethik*. Vol. 6. Edited by Ilse Tödt, Heinz Eduard Tödt, and Ernst Feil. Gütersloh: Gütersloher Verlagshaus, 1998.

Bonhoeffer, Dietrich. *Dietrich Bonhoeffer Werke. Widerstand und Ergebung: Briefe und Aufzeichnungen aus der Haft*. Vol. 8. Edited by Eberhard Bethge. Gütersloh: Chr. Kaiser, 1998.

Bonhoeffer, Dietrich. *Dietrich Bonhoeffer Werke. Konspiration und Haft: 1940-1945*. Vol. 16. Edited by Eberhard Bethge, Jørgen Glenthøj, Ulrich Kabitz, and Wolf Krötke. Gütersloh: Chr. Kaiser, 1996.

Bonhoeffer, Dietrich, *Nachfolge* (Werke 4). Edited by Martin Kuske, and Ilse. Tödt. Gütersloh: Gütersloher Verlagshaus, 2002.

Bonhoeffer, Dietrich. *Dietrich Bonhoeffer Works. Sanctorum Communio: A Theological Study of the Sociology of the Church*. Vol. 1. Edited by Wayne Whitson Floyd Jr. and Clifford J. Green. Minneapolis: Fortress, 2001.

Bonhoeffer, Dietrich. *Dietrich Bonhoeffer Works. Act and Being: A Theological Study of the Sociology of the Church*. Vol. 2. Edited by Wayne Whitson Floyd Jr. Minneapolis: Fortress, 1996.

Bonhoeffer, Dietrich. *Dietrich Bonhoeffer Works. Creation and Fall: A Theological Exposition of Genesis 1-3*. Vol. 3. Edited by Wayne Whitson Floyd, Jr. and John W. De Gruchy. Minneapolis: Fortress, 1997.

Bonhoeffer, Dietrich. *Dietrich Bonhoeffer Works. Discipleship*. Vol. 4. Edited by Wayne Whitson Floyd, Jr., Geffrey B. Kelly, and John D. Godsey. Minneapolis: Fortress, 2001.

Bonhoeffer, Dietrich. *Dietrich Bonhoeffer Works. Life Together and Prayerbook of the Bible*. Vol. 5. Edited by Wayne Whitson Floyd Jr. and Geffrey B. Kelly. Minneapolis: Fortress, 1996.

Bonhoeffer, Dietrich. *Dietrich Bonhoeffer Works. Ethics*. Vol. 6. Edited by Wayne Whitson Floyd Jr. and Clifford J. Green. Minneapolis: Fortress, 2005.

Bonhoeffer, Dietrich. *Dietrich Bonhoeffer Works. Letters and Papers From Prison*. Vol. 8. Edited by Victoria J. Barnett, Barbara Wojhoski, and John W. De Gruchy. Minneapolis: Fortress, 2009.

Bonhoeffer, Dietrich. *Dietrich Bonhoeffer Works. The Young Bonhoeffer: 1918-1927*. Vol. 9. Edited by Wayne Whitson Floyd Jr., Paul Duane Matheny, Clifford J. Green, and Marshall D. Johnson. Minneapolis: Fortress, 2003.

Bibliography

Bonhoeffer, Dietrich. *Dietrich Bonhoeffer Works. Barcelona, Berlin, New York: 1928–1929.* Vol. 10. Edited by Victoria J. Barnett, Barbara Wojhoski, and Clifford J. Green. Minneapolis: Fortress, 2008.

Bonhoeffer, Dietrich. *Dietrich Bonhoeffer Works. Berlin 1932–1933.* Vol. 12. Edited by Victoria J. Barnett, Barbara Wojhoski, and Larry L. Rasmussen. Minneapolis: Fortress, 2009.

Bonhoeffer, Dietrich. *Dietrich Bonhoeffer Works. London: 1933–1935.* Vol. 13. Edited by Victoria J. Barnett, Barbara Wojhoski, and Keith Clements. Minneapolis: Fortress, 2007.

Bonhoeffer, Dietrich. *Dietrich Bonhoeffer Works. Theological Education Underground: 1937–1940.* Vol. 15. Edited by Victoria J. Barnett, Barbara Wojhoski. Minneapolis: Fortress, 2012.

Bonhoeffer, Dietrich. *Dietrich Bonhoeffer Works. Conspiracy and Imprisonment: 1940–1945.* Vol. 16. Edited by Victoria J. Barnett, Wayne Whitson Floyd Jr., Barbara Wojhoski, and Mark S. Brocker. Minneapolis: Fortress, 2006.

Bonhoeffer, Dietrich. *No Rusty Swords: Letters, Lectures, and Notes: 1928–1936.* Collected Works of Dietrich Bonhoeffer. Vol. 1. Edited by Edwin H. Robertson and John Bowden. New York: Harper & Row, 1965.

Brunner, Emil. *Dogmatics Volume 1: The Christian Doctrine of God.* Translated by Olive Wyon. James Clarke & Co., 2002.

Brunner, Emil and Barth, Karl. *Natural Theology: Comprising "Nature and Grace".* Eugene: Wipf & Stock, 2002.

Burtness, James H. *Consequences: Morality, Ethics, and the Future.* Minneapolis: Fortress, 1999.

Burtness, James H. *Shaping the Future: The Ethics of Dietrich Bonhoeffer.* Minneapolis: Augsburg Fortress, 1985.

Carlisle, Clare. *Kierkegaard: A Guide for the Perplexed.* Continuum International Publishing Group, 2006.

Daub, Hans Friedrich. *Die Stellvertretung Jesu Christi: ein Aspekt des Gott-Mensch-Verhältnisses bei Dietrich Bonhoeffer.* Münster: LIT Verlag, 2006.

De Gruchy, John W. *Confessions of a Christian Humanist.* Minneapolis: Fortress, 2006.

De Lange, Frits. "Aristocratic Christendom: On Bonhoeffer and Nietzsche." In *Bonhoeffer and Continental Thought: Cruciform Philosophy.* Edited by Brian Gregor and Jens Zimmerman, 73–83. Bloomington: Indiana University Press, 2009.

Devine, Mark. *Bonhoeffer Speaks Today: Following Jesus at All Costs.* Nashville: Broadman & Holman, 2005.

Dramm, Sabine. *Dietrich Bonhoeffer and the Resistance.* Minneapolis: Fortress, 2009.

Dudzus, Otto. "Arresting the Wheel." In *I Knew Dietrich Bonhoeffer.* Edited by Wolf-Dieter Zimmermann and Ronald Gregor Smith, 82–90. New York: Harper & Row, 1966.

Ericksen, Robert P. *Theologians Under Hitler.* New Haven, CT: Yale University Press, 1987.

Bibliography

Fletcher, Joseph. *Situation Ethics: The New Morality.* Philadelphia: Westminster, 1966.

Floyd, Jr., Wayne Whitson. "Encounter with an Other: Immanuel Kant and G. W. F. Hegel in the Theology of Dietrich Bonhoeffer." In *Bonhoeffer's Intellectual Formation: Theology and Philosophy in his Thought.* Edited by Peter Frick, 83-120. Tübingen: Mohr Siebeck, 2008.

Frame, John M. *Perspectives on the Word of God: An Introduction to Christian Ethics.* Phillipsburg, NJ: Presbyterian and Reformed Publishing Company, 1990.

Fraser, Giles. *Redeeming Nietzsche: on the Piety of Unbelief.* London: Routledge, 2002.

Frick, Peter. "Friedrich Nietzsche's Aphorisms and Dietrich Bonhoeffer's Theology." In *Bonhoeffer's Intellectual Formation: Theology and Philosophy in his Thought.* Edited by Peter Frick, 175-200. Tübingen: Mohr Siebeck, 2008.

Gill, Robin. *A Textbook of Christian Ethics,* 3rd ed. London: T&T Clark, 2006.

Glenthøj, Jørgen. "Dietrich Bonhoeffers Weg vom Pazifismus zum politischen Widerstand." In *Dietrich Bonhoeffer heute: Die Aktualität seines Lebens und Werkes,* 41-57. Basel: Brunnen Verlag Giessen, 1992.

Godsey, John D. *Bonhoeffer for the Eighties: A Report on the Oxford 1980 Conference and an Outlook for the Decade Ahead.* Washington, D.C.: Churches' Center for Theology and Public Policy, 1980), 3.

Godsey, John D. "The Doctrine of Love." In *New Studies in Bonhoeffer's Ethics: Toronto Studies in Theology,* Vol. 30 Bonhoeffer Series no. 3. Edited by William J. Peck, 189-234. New York: The Edwin Mellen Press, 1987.

Godsey, John D. *Preface to Bonhoeffer: The Man and Two of His Shorter Writings.* Philadelphia: Fortress, 1979.

Godsey, John D. "Reading Bonhoeffer in English Translation: Some Difficulties." *Union Seminary Quarterly Review* 23, no. 1 (Fall, 1967): 79-90.

Green, Clifford. "Human sociality and Christian community." In *The Cambridge Companion to Dietrich Bonhoeffer.* Edited by John W. de Gruchy, 115-133. Cambridge: Cambridge University Press, 1999.

Green, Clifford J. *Bonhoeffer: A Theology of Sociality.* Grand Rapids: Wm. B. Eerdmans, 1999.

Green, Clifford J. "Pacifism and Tyrannicide: Bonhoeffer's Christian Peace Ethic." *Studies in Christian Ethics* 18, no. 3 (2005): 31-47.

Green, Clifford J. *The Sociality of Christ and Humanity: Dietrich Bonhoeffer's Early Theology, 1927-1933.* Missoula, MT: Scholar's Press, 1972

Gregor, Brian. "Bonhoeffer's 'Christian Social Philosophy': Conscience, Alterity, and the Moment of Ethical Responsibility." In *Bonhoeffer and Continental Thought: Cruciform Philosophy.* Edited by Brian Gregor and Jans Zimmerman, 201-225. Bloomington: Indiana University Press, 2009.

Griech-Polelle, Beth A. *Bishop von Galen: Roman Catholicism and National Socialism.* New Haven, CT: Yale University Press, 2002.

Bibliography

Guignon, Charles B. and Pereboom, Derk. eds. *Existentialism: Basic Writings*. Indianapolis: Hackett, 2001.

Hampson, Daphne. *Christian Contradictions: The Structures of Lutheran and Catholic Thought*. Cambridge: Cambridge University Press, 2001.

Haynes, Stephen R. *The Bonhoeffer Phenomenon: Portraits of a Protestant Saint*. Minneapolis: Augsburg, 2004.

Hegel, Georg Wilhelm Friedrich. *Early Theological Writings*. Translated by T. M. Knox. Philadelphia: University of Pennsylvania, 1971.

Hetzer, Tanja. *Deutsche Stunde: Volksgemeinschaft und Antisemitismus in der politischen Theologie bei Paul Althaus (Beiträge zur Geschichtswissenschaft)*. München: Buch & Media GmbH, 2009.

Himmler, Heinrich. Speech, November 8, 1938, RFSS/T-175, 90/2612546, The National Archives and Records Service, General Services Administration, Washington, DC, 1961.

Hoffmann, Peter. *The History of the German Resistance: 1933-1945*, 3d ed. Montreal and Kingston: McGill-Queen's University Press, 1996.

Jackson, Timothy P. "Church, World, and Christian Charity." In *Bonhoeffer and King: Their Legacies and Import for Christian Social Thought*. Edited by Willis Jenkins and Jennifer M. McBride, 91-105. Minneapolis: Fortress, 2010.

Kant, Immanuel. *The Conflict of the Faculties*. Translated by Mary Gregor. New York: Abarus Books, 1992.

Kaufmann, Walter. *From Shakespeare to Existentialism*. Princeton, NJ: Princeton University Press, 1980.

Kelly, Geffrey. "Kierkegaard as 'Antidote' and as Impact on Dietrich Bonhoeffer's Concept of Christian Discipleship." In *Bonhoeffer's Intellectual Formation: Theology and Philosophy in his Thought*. Edited by Peter Frick, 145-166. Tübingen: Mohr Siebeck, 2008.

Kelly, Geffrey B. and Nelson, Burton F., eds. *A Testament to Freedom: The Essential Writings of Dietrich Bonhoeffer*. New York: HarperCollins, 1995.

Kelly, Geffrey B. and Nelson, Burton F. *The Cost of Moral Leadership: The Spirituality of Dietrich Bonhoeffer*. Grand Rapids: Wm. B. Eerdmans, 2003.

Krötke, Wolf. "Dietrich Bonhoeffer and Martin Luther." In *Bonhoeffer's Intellectual Formation: Theology and Philosophy in his Thought*. Edited by Peter Frick, 53-82. Tübingen: Mohr Siebeck, 2008.

Lewy, Guenter. "A Secret Papal Brief on Tyrannicide During the Counterreformation." *Church History* 26, no. 4 (December 1957): 319-324.

Lovin, Robin W. *Christian Faith and Public Choices: The Social Ethics of Barth, Brunner, and Bonhoeffer*. Philadelphia: Fortress, 1984.

Lupoi, Maurizio. *The Origins of the European Legal Order*. Cambridge: Cambridge University Press, 2000.

Martin Luther: Die reformatorischen Grundschriften. Gottes Werke und Menschenwerke. Band 1, neu ubertragende und kommentierte *Ausgabe von Horst Beintker*. München: Wissenschaftlichen Buchgesellschaft, 1983.

BIBLIOGRAPHY

May, Simon. *Nietzsche's Ethics and his War on 'Morality'*. Oxford: Oxford University Press, 1999.
MacDonogh, Giles. *1938: Hitler's Gamble*. New York: Basic Books, 2011.
Mayes, Benjamin T. G. *Counsel and Conscience: Lutheran Casuistry and Moral Reasoning After the Reformation*. Göttingen: Vandenhoeck & Ruprecht GmbH & Co. KG, 2011.
Mikkelsen, Hans Vium. *Reconciled Humanity: Karl Barth in Dialogue*. Cambridge: Wm. B. Eerdmans, 2010.
Miller, Richard Brian. *Casuistry and Modern Ethics: A Poetics of Practical Reasoning*. Chicago: The University of Chicago Press, 1996.
Moe-Lobeda, Cynthia. "A Theology of the Cross for the 'Uncreators.'" In *Cross Examinations: Readings on the Meaning of the Cross Today*. Edited by Marit Trelstad, 181–195. Minneapolis: Augsburg Fortress, 2006.
Moltmann, Jürgen. "The Lordship of Christ and Human Society." In *Two Studies in the Theology of Bonhoeffer*. Translated by Reginald H. Fuller and Ilse Fuller, 19–94. New York: Charles Scribner's Sons, 1967.
Moses, John Anthony. *The Reluctant Revolutionary: Dietrich Bonhoeffer's Collision with Prusso-German History*. New York: Berghahn Books, 2009.
Müller, Hanfried. *Von der Kirche zur Welt*. Hamburg: Herbert Reich Evang. Verlag GmbH, 1961.
Nickson, Ann L. *Bonhoeffer on Freedom: Courageously Grasping Reality*. England: Ashgate, 2002.
Nietzsche, Friedrich. *The Anti-Christ, Ecce Homo, Twilight of the Idols and Other Writings*. Edited by Aaron Ridley and Judith Norman. Cambridge: Cambridge University Press, 2005.
Nietzsche, Friedrich. *Beyond Good and Evil*. Edited by Rolf-Peter Horstmann and Judith Norman. Cambridge: Cambridge University Press, 2002.
Nietzsche, Friedrich. *Daybreak: Thoughts on the Prejudices of Morality*. Edited by Maudemarie Clark and Brian Leiter. Cambridge: Cambridge University Press, 1997.
Nietzsche, Friedrich. *The Gay Science*. Edited by Bernard Williams. Cambridge: Cambridge University Press, 2001.
Nolzen, Armin. *Germany and the Second World War: Germany Wartime Society 1939-1945: Politicization, Disintegration, and the Struggle for Survival*, Vol. IX/I. Oxford: Oxford University Press, 2008.
Oh, Peter S. *Karl Barth's Trinitarian Theology: A Study in Karl Barth's Analogical Use of the Trinitarian Relation*. London: T&T Clark, 2006.
Ott, Heinrich. *Wirklichkeit und Glaube*. Zurich: Vandenhoeck und Ruprecht, 1966.
Pangritz, Andreas. "Dietrich Bonhoeffer: 'Within not Outside the Barthian Movement.'" In *Bonhoeffer's Intellectual Formation: Theology and Philosophy in his Thought*. Edited by Peter Frick, 245–282. Tübingen: Mohr Siebeck, 2008.
Pierard, Richard V. "The Lutheran Two-Kingdoms Doctrine and Subservience to the State in Modern Germany." *JETS* 29, no. 2 (June 1986): 193–203.

Bibliography

Plant, Stephen. *Bonhoeffer*. Continuum, 2004.
Plaskow, Judith. *The Coming of Lilith: Essays on Feminism, Judaism, and Sexual Ethics, 1972-2003*. Edited by Donna Berman. Boston: Beacon, 2005.
Rades, Jörg Alfred. Draft Chapters for a Bonhoeffer dissertation, University of St. Andrews, Scotland ca. 1986-1989. "Luther and Bonhoeffer" [c.1983-1989] University of St. Andrews, Scotland. UTS Archives, Bonhoeffer Secondary Papers, Series 2A Box 3.
Rades, Jörg Alfred. Draft Chapters for a Bonhoeffer dissertation, University of St. Andrews, Scotland ca. 1986-1989. "Nietzsche and Bonhoeffer" Second Draft. [c. 1983-1989] University of St. Andrews, Scotland. UTS Archives, Bonhoeffer Secondary Papers, Series 2A Box 3.
Rasmussen, Larry L. "A Question of Method." In *New Studies in Bonhoeffer's Ethics: Toronto Studies in Theology, Vol. 30: Bonhoeffer Series no. 3*. Edited by William J. Peck, 103-140. New York: The Edwin Mellen Press, 1987.
Rasmussen, Larry L. *Dietrich Bonhoeffer: Reality and Resistance*. Louisville: Westminster John Knox, 2005.
Retter, Ralf. *Theological-Political Resistance: the Role of Dietrich Bonhoeffer and Hans-Bernd von Haeften in the German Resistance Against Hitler*. Berlin: Logos Verlag Berlin GmbH, 2008.
Roberts, James Deotis. *Bonhoeffer and King: Speaking Truth to Power*. Louisville: Westminster John Knox, 2005.
Robertson, Edwin H. and Bowden, John. *No Rusty Swords: Letters, Lectures, and Notes: 1926-1936*. New York: Harper & Row, 1965.
Robertson, Edwin. *The Shame and the Sacrifice: The Life and Martyrdom of Dietrich Bonhoeffer*. New York: MacMillan, 1988.
Rothuizen, Gerard Th. "Who Am I? Bonhoeffer and Suicide." Translated by Edwin Robertson and William J. Peck. In *New Studies in Bonhoeffer's Ethics: Toronto Studies in Theology, Vol. 30: Bonhoeffer Series no. 3*. Edited by William J. Peck, 167-188. New York: The Edwin Mellen Press, 1987.
Rumscheidt, Martin. "The Significance of Adolf von Harnack and Reinhold Seeberg for Dietrich Bonhoeffer." In *Bonhoeffer's Intellectual Formation: Theology and Philosophy in his Thought*. Edited by Peter Frick, 201-224. Tubingen: Mohr Siebeck, 2008.
Runestam, Arvid. "Die Nachfolge Jesu," *Zeitschrift für systematische Theologie* 6 (1929): 747-775.
Sanchez, Allejandro Cavallazzi, and Sanchez, Azucena Palavicini. "Jean Wahl: Philosophies of Existence and the Introduction of Kierkegaard in the non-Germanic World." In *Kierkegaard and Existentialism, Kierkegaard Research: Sources, Reception and Resources*. Vol. 9. Edited by Jon Stewart, 393-414. Farnham: Ashgate, 2011.
Seeberg, Reinhold. *Christliche Dogmatik*. Vol. 2. Erlangen-Leipzig: A. Deichertsch Verlagsbuchhandlung, 1852.
Seeberg, Reinhold. *The Fundamental Truths of the Christian Religion: Sixteen Lectures delivered in the University of Berlin during the Winter Term*

BIBLIOGRAPHY

1901-2. Translated by George E. Thomson and Clara Wallentin. New York: G. P. Putnam's Sons, 1908.

Schlingensiepen, Ferdinand. *Dietrich Bonhoeffer, 1906-1945: Martyr, Thinker, Man of Resistance*. T&T Clark International, 2010.

Smith, Roger L. *The Existential Posture: A Christian Look at its Meaning, Impact, Values, and Dangers*. New York: Association Press, 1970.

Smith, Gerald Birney. "The Modern-Positive Movement in Theology." *The American Journal of Theology* 13, no. 1 (1909): 92-99.

Smith, Ronald Gregor, ed. *World Come of Age: A Symposium on Dietrich Bonhoeffer*. London: Collins, 1967.

Smith, Woodruff D. *The Ideological Origins of Nazi Imperialism*. Oxford: Oxford University Press, 1989.

Stackelberg, Roderick. *Idealism Debased: From Völkisch Ideology to National Socialism*. Kent, OH: The Kent State University Press, 1981.

Tödt, Heinz Eduard. *Authentic Faith: Bonhoeffer's Theological Ethics in Context*. Edited by Ernst-Albert Scharffenorth and Glen Harold Stassen. Grand Rapids: Wm. B. Eerdmans, 2007.

Verhey, Jeffrey. *The Spirit of 1914: Militarism, Myth, and Mobilization in Germany*. Cambridge: Cambridge University Press, 2004.

Vogel, Heinrich Traugott. *Christus als Vorbild und Versöhner: eine Kritische Studie zum Problem der Verhältnisse von Gesetz und Evangelium im Werke Sören Kierkegaards*. Berlin: Humboldt-Universität, 1968.

Volf, Miroslav. *Exclusion and Embrace: a Theological Exploration of Identity, Otherness, and Reconciliation*. Nashville: Abingdon, 1996.

Wannenwetsch, Bernd. "'Responsible Living or 'Responsible Self'? Bonhoefferian Reflections on a Vexed Moral Notion." *Studies in Christian Ethics* 18, no. 3 (2005): 125-140.

Wannenwetsch, Bernd. *Who Am I? Bonhoeffer's Theology through his Poetry*. London: T&T Clark, 2009.

Webster, John Bainbridge, ed. *The Cambridge Companion to Karl Barth*. Cambridge: Cambridge University Press, 2000.

Weikart, Richard. "Metaxas' Counterfeit Bonhoeffer: An Evangelical Critique." http://www.csustan.edu/history/faculty/weikart/metaxas.htm (accessed March 12, 2012).

Weikart, Richard. "So Many Different Bonhoeffers." *Trinity Journal* 32, NS (2011): 69-81.

Weikart, Richard. *The Myth of Dietrich Bonhoeffer: Is His Theology Evangelical?* San Francisco: International Scholars Publications, 1997. 105.

Weinberg, Gerhard L. *Hitler's Foreign Policy 1933-1939: The Road to World War II*. New York: Enigma Books, 2005.

Weissbach, Jürgen. "Christology and Ethics." In *Two Studies in the Theology of Bonhoeffer*, translated by Reginald H. Fuller and Ilse Fuller, 95-148. New York: Charles Scribner's Sons, 1967.

Bibliography

Wiley, Craig. "I was Dead and Behold, I am Alive Forevermore: Responses to Nietzsche in 20th Century Christian Theology." *Intersections* 10, no. 1 (2009): 507–517.

Williams, Rowan. "Bonhoeffer, the Sixties, and After: Consultation on Bonhoeffer: Britain and British Theology." Paper presented at the Conference of the International Bonhoeffer Society, British Section, January 1991. UTS Archives, Bonhoeffer Secondary Papers, Series 1B Box 5.

Willmer, Haddon. "Costly Discipleship." In *The Cambridge Companion to Dietrich Bonhoeffer*. Edited by John W. de Gruchy, 173–189. Cambridge: Cambridge University Press, 1999.

Wind, Renate. *Dietrich Bonhoeffer: A Spoke in the Wheel*. Grand Rapids: Wm. B. Eerdmans, 2002.

Woelfel, James W. *Bonhoeffer's Theology: Classical and Revolutionary*. Nashville: Abingdon, 1970.

Wright, William John. *Martin Luther's Understanding of God's Two Kingdoms: A Response to the Challenge of Skepticism*. Grand Rapids: Baker Academic, 2010.

Zimmerman, Wolf-Dieter. "Years in Berlin." In *I Knew Dietrich Bonhoeffer*. Edited by Wolf-Dieter Zimmermann and Ronald Gregor Smith, 59–67. New York: Harper & Row, 1966.

Index

Act and Being (Bonhoeffer), xvii, 26, 50
action
   as sociological mode of the church, 23
   value of, 25
Agricola, 25
Alemany, José J., 133
Althaus, Paul, 27n100, 110–11n19
Ansbach Reply, 7, 54n64
Anselm, 23
anthropological question, 49
Anti-Christ, The (Nietzsche), 15
applied theology, 89
Aquinas, Thomas, 23, 105n120
atomism, 43, 47–48
atonement theology, 4
Attack upon Christendom (Kierkegaard), 9
Augenblick (Kierkegaard), 9
Augustine, 9, 23

Bagetto, Luca, 13
Barmen Declaration, 7
Barth, Karl, xvi, xvii, 4, 9, 27–30, 52, 117, 126, 130, 140n101
being-for-the-person, 6, 52
belief, 47
Bell, George K. A., 72
Bentham, Jeremy, 37–38

Bethge, Eberhard, 4–5, 19, 26, 27, 28, 32–34, 86, 90, 95, 97, 100, 113, 115
Biggar, Nigel, 41
Bonhoeffer, Dietrich
   affection of, for sensate, 44
   analysis of 1 Clement, 44–45
   on atonement, 4
   Barth's influence on, 27–30
   on casuistry, 41–43
   censorship of, 92–93
   Christological ethics of, 53, 56, 126. See also Bonhoeffer, ethics of
   Christology of, 44, 52, 58, 141, 144
   and commandment-based living, 12
   committed to the individual, 118
   on community, 52, 55, 98–99, 117–18
   as contradiction of nationalistic thinker, 115–16n25
   concern of, for students, 96–98
   as conspirator in plot to kill Hitler, 121–28, 130
   constructive theology of, 45–46
   contempt of, for fellow prisoners at Tegel, 17

Index

Bonhoeffer, Dietrich (continued)
contextual ethics of, 35, 40
contextualism of, 60, 87, 94
on dogmatics and ethics as unified, 4
ecumenism of, 53, 74–75, 85–88, 135
ethical methodology of, 31, 39, 44–49, 89, 101, 109, 144
ethics of, 67, 116, 120
as existentialist thinker, 34–35
on genuine Christian thinkers, 9
on grace, 12–13
on Grisebach, 51
on guilt, 132–43
on Heidegger, 50, 51
on the incarnation, 4
influence of, on Christianity, xv
influences on, 1–30
interested in other religions, 78
interpreting secular life theologically, 8
on judging, 73–74
Kierkegaard's influence on, 8–14, 30
liberation of, 83–84
on the Lord's Supper, 5–6
Luther's influence on, 1–8, 17, 30, 116
methodological approach of, 121. See also Bonhoeffer, ethical methodology of
on military service, 95–99
moving into ethics, 108
on murder, 123
in New York City, 77–80
Nietzsche's influence on, 15–21, 30
on normative ethical thinking, 134
obedience in ethics of, 61–64
overcoming disunion of good and evil, 19n76

on pacifism, 81
pacifism of, xvii–xix, 68–69, 79, 85–87, 106
on peace, 66–67, 73, 80–88. See also peace
in process of forgiving and reconciling, 73
rejecting deontological ethics, 32–33
rejection of, xv–xvi
relationship as central to, 105
on religionless Christianity, 21
on renunciation, 90–91
on responsibility, 129–32
resistance activities of, 30, 96, 98, 123
on retribution, doctrine of, 93–94
on sacramental Christology, 5
on Scheler, 50
Seeberg's influence on, 21–27, 30
and the Sermon on the Mount, 80, 83, 107, 109
sermons of, 112–13, 115
on sin, 116–17, 132–43
on suffering, 138–39
suicidal tendencies of, 17n66
on suicide, 113–14n21
theologia crucis and, 92, 94
theology of, xvii, 98, 103, 117
on theory of the Person, 49–51
on Tillich, 50
translating Luther's doctrines as ethical interpretations, 3
on utilitarianism, 38
on war, rejection of, 85–87, 99–100
Bonhoeffer, Emmi, 124–25
Brocker, Mark S., 130
Brunner, Emil, xvii, 23, 140n101
Bultmann, Rudolf, xvii, 52
Burtness, James H., 143

Index

casuistry, 41–43
Catullus, 44
Celsus, 15
cheap grace, 12, 29, 89n72
Christ
  becoming humanity, 52, 56n73
  as being-for-others, 52, 137
  at center of human activity, 53
  embracing humanity, 141
  as ethical reality of creation, 57
  ethical reflection and, 36
  as ground of the church, 53
  obedience in, 82
  occupying real historical space, 60
  presence of, 55
  as reality, 43, 58–59, 101–2
  redemptive mode of, 117
  relationship in, 70, 81
  sinlessness of, 140–41, 143
  submission to, 61
Christian ethics, 16
Christianity
  Nietzsche on, 15–16, 18–21
  religionless, 59
Christian love, 73–74, 101
Christiche Dogmatik (Seeberg), 22, 26
Christology, 31, 44
Christus als Vorbild und Versöhner (Vogel), 12
Christus praesens, 6, 53, 54, 55
church
  authority of, 53
  task of, 99
Church Dogmatics (Barth), 28, 29–30
Church and the New Order, The (Paton), 130
Clement, Keith W., xv
command, obedience and, 28–30
commandment ethics, 39
commandments, 32, 36–37, 47, 49, 54, 86, 100

Communio Sanctorum (Althaus), 27n100
community, 13, 26, 117–18
  Bonhoeffer's emphasis on, 34, 37, 51
  destruction of, 94
  individuals and, 52, 118, 132, 141
community of saints, 14
concretion, 28, 35, 47, 114
Confessing Church, 12, 14, 57, 118
conscientious objection, 96–97
constructive theology, 45–46
contemplation, 23
context, 47
contextualism, 23, 60
Council of Constance, 125
creation, story of, 88
Creation and Fall: A Theological Exposition of Genesis (Bonhoeffer), 13, 26, 49, 61–62, 88, 129
creationism, 117

Dasein (being-there), 50, 53
Dasein-für-andere, 52–53
Daub, Hans Friedrich, 3, 4
De Gruchy, John W., 97, 129–30
De Lange, Fritz, 15, 17, 18
deontological ethics, 32–34, 37
Der Einzelne und die Kirche (Kierkegaard), 12
Devine, Mark, 88
dialectical theology, 27
discipleship, ethics and, 88–89
Discipleship (Bonhoeffer), 3, 8n32, 29, 56n72, 61, 62, 80–81, 82, 88–95, 103, 120, 127
divine attributes, 5
divine simplicity, 105n120
Dudzus, Otto, 80n46, 114

ecumenical movement, 85–88
ecumenism, 74–75

Index

enemies
    encountering with love, 93, 103
    praying for, 82, 93
Epictetus, 15
Epicureanism, 38
epistemology, 22
Ericksen, Robert, 27
ethical collective person, 116–20
ethical rationalism, 41
ethical universal, 69
ethics
    Barth and Bonhoeffer's discussions on, 27
    as command, 27n28
    deontological, 32–34, 37
    discipleship and, 88–89
    doing of, 35
    existential, 34–35, 37
    history and, 33
    individuality and, 11
    Nietzsche's approach to, 18–19
    relationship and, 13, 44
    and the relationship with God, 9–10
    situational, 35–37
    suspension of, 11
    universality of, 10–11
Ethics (Bonhoeffer), 8, 17, 29, 39, 42, 55, 56–61, 82, 123–24, 129–31, 136–37
Ethik als Gebot (command), 39–40, 43, 59–60
Ethik als Gestalt (formation), 39–40, 43, 59–60
evil, ethical category of, 61
existential ethics, 34–35, 37
existentialism, 51

faith, 3n9, 102, 103
    Bonhoeffer's understanding of, 12
    independent from political life, 7
    obedience and, 62
    primacy of, 10
    private, 14
family, defense of, 110, 113
Faust (Goethe), 76–77
Fear and Trembling (Kierkegaard), 10
Finkenwalde, seminary at, 96, 98
Fisher, Frank, 78
Fletcher, Joseph, 35, 36, 42
formalism, 41
Frame, John, 34
Fraser, Giles, 18
freedom, 13, 56, 63–64
    church birthed in, 20
    obedience and, 129
    responsibility and, 129–32
Frick, Peter, 17
friedlos, 76n31

Galen, Clemens August Count von, 72–73
Genesis, story of, 49, 88
German theology, 22
Germany
    Luther's influence on, 1–2
    and the Treaty of Versailles, 70–71
    two kingdoms doctrine in, 7
    under Nazism, 120
    after World War I, 70–73, 119
Gestalt ethics, 40
Gill, Robin, 36
Glenthøj, Jørgen, 87
God
    attributes of, 105–6
    encounters with, 48
    reality of, 102
    relationship with, 12, 67
    right response to, 25
    self-revelation of, 104
    speaking, 14
Godsey, John D., xv, xvii, xix–xx, 27n100, 85–86, 88
Goethe, Johann Wolfgang von, 76

INDEX

Gogarten, Friedrich, 51
good, ethical category of, 61
grace, 11, 12, 35, 48-49. See also
  cheap grace
  ethics and, 27
  works and, 29
Green, Clifford J., 3-4, 38, 41n28,
  55-56, 68, 76, 80, 102, 103,
  110-11, 116, 118, 125-28,
  134, 140
Grisebach, Eberhard, 49-50
Guignon, Charles, 11-12
guilt, 132-43

Hampson, Daphne, 6
Harnack, Adolf von, 22
Hase, Hans Christop von, 84, 85
Havenstein, Martin, 16-17
Haynes, Stephen R., xv, 107-8
Heckel, Theodor, 92n80
Hegel, G. W. F., 11
Heidegger, Martin, 20, 49-50, 51, 53
Hildebrandt, Franz, 80, 111
Hillel, 37
Himmler, Heinrich, 71
history
  ethics and, 33
  revelation and, 24
Hitler, Adolf
  assassination plot against, xv, xviii, 121-28, 130
  compared with Jesus, 7
  resistance to, 71
  rising to Chancellery, 83
  theologians' reaction to, 27
Hoffmann, Peter C., 72
Horace, 44
humanness, question of, 49

idealism, 18-19, 44, 104, 128
inauthenticity, 20
incarnation, 4, 56-57
individuality, 11-12, 18, 99

individuals, community and, 118, 132, 141
intrapersonal relationships, importance of, 34-35
isolation, 13

Jackson, Timothy P., 104
Jesus, on murder, 120-21
Jordan, Hermann, 7
Journey's End (Sheriff), 79-80
Jugendbewegung, 9

Kanitz, Joachim, 97-98
Kant, Immanuel, 10, 17
Kaufmann, Walter, 14
Kelly, Geffrey B., xv, 8, 9, 12, 13, 85-86, 88, 137
kenosis, 5
Kierkegaard, Søren, 6, 8-14, 21, 27n101, 30, 34-35, 69
Kirchliche Dogmatik (Barth). See *Church Dogmatics* (Barth)
Kollectivperson, 13-14, 23. See also ethical collective person
Kranz, Walther, 44
Krauss, Reinhard, 134

Lasserre, Jean, 77-78, 79, 87
Lebensraum, 58
Lehmann, Paul, 78
Leibholz, Gerhard, 99
Lord's Supper, 5-6, 31
love
  Christian, 36-37, 73-74, 101
  as greatest good, 82-83
  peace and, 101-3
  relational ethics and, 101-6
  tied to God's revelation in Jesus, 104
Lovin, Robin W., 63n94
Lütgert, Wilhelm, 26
Luther, Martin, 1-8, 9, 17, 25, 30, 42, 52, 87, 133
  influence of, on Bonhoeffer, 116

161

Index

Luther, Martin (continued)
   on the Lord's Supper, 5
   rejecting transubstantiation, 6
   on two kingdoms, 6–7
Lyman, Eugene William, 103

mandates, 40
May, Simon, 18
Mayes, Benjamin T. G., 41n28
Menschwerdung, 52, 56, 117, 131
methodological atomism, 47–48
Miller, Richard Brian, 42
Moltmann, Jürgen, 40
moral character, 25
morality, Christian monopoly on, 19
Moses, John Anthony, 38, 135
Müller, Hanfried, 40
murder, 12, 120–25
   commandment against, 110
   Jesus' rejection of, 120–21
   peace and, 107–8
   tyrannicide distinct from, 125–28
   war and, 118–20

Nachlass Dietrich Bonhoeffer, 90
nationalism, 26
Nazism (National Socialism), 6–7, 30, 112
Nelson, Burton, 137
Nickson, Ann L., xvii
Nietzsche, Friedrich, 15–21, 30, 34–35, 76–77
nonviolence, pacifism and, 66, 68
Novatian, 134n81

obedience, 56, 61–64, 82, 86, 131–32
   command and, 28–30
   freedom and, 129
Olbricht, Fritz, 112–13n19
Oppel, Frances Nesbitt, 77
other, encounter with, 51

Ott, Heinrich, 43

pacifism
   Bonhoeffer's, xvii–xix, 88
   conspiracy and, xviii
   nonviolence and, 66, 68
   peace distinguished from, 103
   practice of, 67
   provisional, 70, 99, 106, 111
   and renunciation of violence, 90–91
   subject to Christ, 69
Pangritz, Andreas, 29
Paton, William, 130
Paul, 9, 15
peace
   Bonhoeffer's definition of, 70–77
   Bonhoeffer's quest for, 66
   call to, 80
   commandment to, 81, 87–88
   conceived in Christ's love for humanity, 81
   distinguished from pacifism, 103
   God as ground of, 75–76
   love and, 82–83, 101–3
   methodological approach to, 67
   murder and, 107–8
   provisional, 68
   self-evident nature of, 69
   starting point of, 67
   theme of, 32, 68
   transitory expressions of, 76
   types of, 75, 81–82
peacemakers
   job of, 82
   suffering of, 92–93
Pereboom, Derk, 11–12
Person, concept of, 49
philosophy, 52
Pierard, Richard B., 7, 8, 54n64
pious, Socratic problem of, 69

Index

Plant, Stephen, 10, 33
Plaskow, Judith, xvi
Plato, 76, 77n34
positive theology, 22
Prayerbook of the Bible, The (Bonhoeffer), 141–42
principle-based thinking, 41
principles, 43
   for living, 33–34
   usefulness of, 42
Problema I, 11

Rades, Jörg, 2–3, 5, 17
Rasmussen, Larry, xv, xviii, xix, 14, 27–30, 35, 39–43, 47–48, 59–60, 85, 87, 100, 101, 111, 129, 137
rationalism, 30
reconciliation, 73, 75, 81–82
redemption, 117
Reinsdorf Theses, 7
relational-Christological ethics, 39–43
relational ethics, 49, 101–6, 144
relationships, 12–13, 44, 48, 105
religion, nature of, 26
religious determinism, 48
religious tribalism, 30
renunciation, 90–91
representation, incarnation and, 4
responsibility, 56, 63, 129–32
responsible action, context for, 135
retribution, doctrine of, 93–94
revelation, 45–46, 51–52
   history and, 24
   shared experience of, 31
Riemer, Gerhard, 55
Roberts, James Deotis, 10
Robertson, Edwin H., 70–71, 86, 115
Rothuizen, Gerard Th., 139
Rumscheidt, Martin, 1, 22–24
Runestam, Arvid, 89

saints, community of, 14
salvation, 18n68
Sanctorum Communio (Bonhoeffer), 5–6, 9, 22, 51, 52, 69–70, 83, 84, 112–13n19, 116, 118n33, 133, 140
Scheler, Max, 49–50
Schlingensiepen, Ferdinand, 122, 124
scientific outlook, 46–47
Seeberg, Reinhold, 21–27, 30, 101, 116, 119n
selfhood, slavery of, 63–64
Seneca, 37
Sermon on the Mount, 109
Sheriff, Robert C., 79–80
Shinn, Roger L., 14
simplicitas Dei, 23
sin, 11, 12, 116–17, 132–43
   composition of, 24–25
   forgiveness of, 5, 136
   individual, 13–14, 117, 140
   as ontological concept, 117, 135
   original, 26, 117, 133–34, 140
situation ethics, 35–37
Smith, Gerald Birney, 22n85
Smith, Woodruff D., 112
social realism, 23
Sociality of Christ and Humanity, The (Green), 117
Staats, Reinhart, 18, 71, 79
Stackelberg, Roderick, 111–12
Stellvertretung, 3–4, 140, 141
suffering, 92, 138–39, 142
suicide, 113–14n21
Sutz, Erwin, 27, 78

Tegel, Bonhoeffer's actions at, 17
theological anthropology, 52
theology. *See also* Bonhoeffer, theology of
   dialectical, 27

Index

theology (continued)
  German, 22
  In Principiis approach to, 46
  modern-positive approach to, 24
Thus Spoke Zarathustra (Nietzsche), 76–77
Tillich, Paul, 49–50, 76n33
Tödt, Heins Eduard, 2, 4, 19n76, 22, 93, 110, 111
traducianism, 117
transcendence, 21–22, 23, 54
transcendentalism, 22
transubstantiation, 6
Treaty of Versailles, 70–71
two kingdoms, doctrine of, 6–8
tyrannicide, 125–28

Union Theological Seminary (New York), 78–79, 84n56
universalism, Christian, 59–60
utilitarianism, 37–38

Verantwortung, 56n72, 129, 130
violence, renunciation of, 90–91
Visser 't Hooft, W. A., xvii
Vogel, Heinrich Traugott, 3n9, 12
Volf, Miroslav, xviii
völkisch ideology, 111–12, 114–16, 118–19

Volksgemeinschaft, 74
voluntarism, 22, 24
Von Haeften, Werner, 124, 128
Von Wedemeyer, Hans, 97
Von Wedemeyer, Maria, 97

Wannenwetsch, Bernd, 129, 130
war, murder and, 118–20
Weikart, Richard, xvi
Weltlichkeit, 67
Widmann, Richard, 9
Wiley, Craig, 16
will
  as God's primary mode, 23
  moral character and, 25
Williams, Rowan, xvi
Willmer, Haddon, 29
Wind, Renate, 96
Wise, Stephen, 79
Word, high Christology of, 57
World Alliance for Promoting International Friendship through the Churches, 67–68n3, 85
Wright, William John, 6–7

Zimmerman, Wolf-Dieter, 113n, 124, 128

www.ingramcontent.com/pod-product-compliance
Lightning Source LLC
Chambersburg PA
CBHW071449150426
43191CB00008B/1285